# ROUGH WAYS IN PRAYER

Paul Wallis was born in 1965 in Buckinghamshire. Before training for ministry at St John's College, Nottingham, he was Pastoral Assistant at St George the Martyr in central London and at The City University. This involved him in pastoral care, worship leading, preaching and taking people on retreat. He has travelled widely and is a keen musician. He is now a curate at a church in Camden Town, London.

PAUL WALLIS

# Rough Ways
# in Prayer

### HOW CAN I PRAY
### WHEN I FEEL SPIRITUALLY DEAD?

*Foreword by*
*JOYCE HUGGETT*

First published 1991
Triangle
SPCK
Holy Trinity Church
Marylebone Road
London NW1 4DU

Unless otherwise indicated, all Bible quotations are taken from the *New International Version*, copyright © 1973, 1978, 1984 by the International Bible Society. Published by Hodder & Stoughton.
Other versions used are the Jerusalem Bible (JB), New Jerusalem Bible (NJB) – both published by Darton, Longman and Todd – New American Standard Bible (NASB) and Revised Standard Version (RSV).

Metropolitan Anthony quotations are taken from *The Essence of Prayer*, copyright © 1986 by Darton, Longman and Todd, and are used by kind permission of the publishers.

British Library Cataloguing in Publication Data
Wallis, Paul *1965–*
Rough ways in prayer.
1. Christian life. Prayer
I. Title
248.32

ISBN 0-281-04483-X

Typeset by Inforum Typesetting, Portsmouth
Printed in Great Britain by
BPCC Hazell Books
Aylesbury, Bucks
Member of BPCC Ltd.

# Contents

*This book is dedicated*
*to Phil*

# Foreword

I was suffering from jet lag when the postman delivered the manuscript of *Rough Ways in Prayer*. I had just returned from a teaching tour of New Zealand and within a week was to exchange the wide open spaces for a hospital bed in London where I was to undergo major surgery.

In other words, I felt completely disorientated—disinclined to read yet another book on prayer. But I had promised the author that I would read what he had written so, dutifully, I turned to the Preface. 'It will have to be good to grip me at this moment in time,' I murmured to myself as I began to read. The first few sentences hooked me:

Sometimes prayer is simple.
Sometimes it seems impossible . . .
How can I pray when I feel dry and dead?

Perhaps the manuscript would speak into my disorientation and its consequent spiritual apathy?

It did. I found it impossible to read the pages in the slow, meditative manner I usually adopt when I read books on prayer. The contents were so readable, so practical and, at times, so profound, that I romped to the end as fast as I could. By that time I felt full of hope. The book had reminded me of certain significant insights: that 'it is those who are alive who are concerned about deadness', that we must not make the mistake of believing that our feelings are a barometer of our love for God, that dryness in prayer may be the result of a bereavement, retirement, ill health, that the way to come to God is just as we are— confused, happy, sad . . .

Such timely reminders restored a much needed sense of perspective. Prayer was becoming easy once more. The days leading up to my operation were memorable because the sense of God's loving presence was powerful.

After the operation, however, everything changed. My mind refused to function, my emotions seemed still to be anaesthetized, my body was weak, my imagination went on strike, my senses seemed numb and my appetite for prayer shrivelled. For weeks I was to stumble through the spiritual desert—that trackless waste where it is easy to lose one's bearings.

I turned to the manuscript again, this time, not from duty but in desperation. It became my constant companion and it gave me the courage to struggle on for two reasons: first, it gave me the assurance I needed that the desert is the place where God often effects profound changes, and second because the author provides a series of user-friendly spiritual exercises which he suggests his readers use when all that spreads before them is the howling wilderness. I experimented with these exercises and found that, over a period of months, first one and then another brought me to the realization that, although I could neither hear nor feel God, my commitment to him was as strong as ever. This reassurance lightened my sense of desolation.

Having used the book as a life-line for myself, I began to look at the manuscript more objectively. Would it encourage the woman who had confessed to me, 'When my mother died, I was devastated. I found myself completely unable to draw on my faith'? Would it help the girl who comes to me for spiritual direction and who is searching for a few landmarks as she stumbles through the desert for the first time? Would it inspire the couple who keep confessing to me that they are in the spiritual pits? I thought of some of the superb quotations the book contains—from St Bernard, Christians from the Orthodox tradition and present day writers like Kenneth Leech. I thought, too, of the refreshing breadth of spirituality which blows through the book like a breeze on a humid day and I thought of the positive definitions of the spiritual desert which the author gives and I felt confident that this strangely joyful book would be welcomed by each of these individuals and many like them; people who anxiously seek for an answer to that question: 'How *can* I pray when I feel spiritually dead?'

Others will value this book too—particularly those who have the privilege of giving spiritual direction to others. We are not protected from the spiritual waste-lands as I, myself, have experienced on several occasions. Perhaps we are more conscious than most that Bishop Theophan's observation is painfully accurate: 'Most people are like a shaving of wood which is curled round its emptiness.' When we are so conscious of our own inner emptiness that a prayer like the Jesus Prayer becomes an urgent *cri de coeur*, then we may find ourselves cast back upon the author's user-friendly exercises for a while.

And even if we never have to resort to these exercises for ourselves, when others describe for us that inner ache which Pascal once called the 'God-shaped gap', having read this important book, we shall be able to reassure them that the desert can become a meeting place with the living God; that it often proves to be a place into which God lures his people in order that he may share with them secrets which cannot be disclosed when all in the spiritual garden seems to be lovely. We shall be better equipped to journey with others through the darkness. And we shall be able to place into their hands *Rough Ways in Prayer* confident that it will help them to pray even when prayer seems absolutely impossible.

JOYCE HUGGETT

# Preface

Sometimes prayer is simple.
Sometimes it seems impossible.
Sometimes the life of prayer is fulfilling and refreshing.
Other times it's dry and lifeless.
How can I pray when I feel dry and dead? How can I keep
prayer going when I'm in a spiritual desert? Like the exiled
Jews of the Old Testament, 'How can I sing the Lord's
song in a strange land?'

Like the Jews, exiled in Babylon, are you fed up and
cheesed off? Disillusioned in prayer or in the faith itself?
Bored and unenthused? It may be that praying doesn't
seem to work any more and that your life of prayer is just
about ready to peter out.

If so, then read on. This book is not going to make all
your problems magically disappear with a flick of a wrist.
But I hope that it can give you some new help, some new
inspiration and encouragement. You will find yourself in
good company!

# PART 1

*Therefore gird your minds for action, keep sober in spirit, fix your hope completely on the grace to be brought to you at the revelation of Christ Jesus.*

1 PETER 1.13 NASB

# Introduction

The Christian life is a battlefield. The people to whom St Peter wrote these words were just beginning to find this out. Temptation, conflicts of allegiance and ambition, hardship, tiredness, busyness and boredom all conspire against the Christian life. And the recipients of Peter's letter were just beginning to encounter real persecution. For St Peter's readers, both then and now, the Christian life means battle.

Before he embarks on instructing his readers Peter first tells us that we must have minds 'prepared for action'. Translations such as the NASB keep to the imagery of Peter's own language, using phrases such as 'gird your minds' or, more literally, 'having girt the loins of your mind'. Sadly, however, the metaphor is lost on the modern reader. The image is that of someone wearing first-century Middle-Eastern robes, gathering them up around his knees so that he can run without tripping himself up. Peter is saying that if we are to take on board what he is saying and live it out effectively, we must do the mental equivalent of that, otherwise we'll trip ourselves up. This means getting our thinking straight. It means having an appropriate 'mind-set'.

Anthony de Mello tells of an anonymous tribe where the highest judicial punishment administered is that of banishment. The guilty party is simply banished from the tribe and almost invariably dies within a few days. The question is, what is it that kills the person? Ostracism in itself does not have the power to kill. What kills the man is his culturally programmed reaction to the punishment. For him, being ostracized is the worst thing that can happen: it is life-destroying. That is what he has learned to think. It is an unquestioned part of his mind-set. And it is that which kills him—not the ostracism itself!

In order to survive the spiritual desert, we need to take control of our thinking and our whole mind-set. To survive, we need to learn the art of thinking differently. If we are to endure the desert experience, we must review and reappraise our whole way of seeing and thinking. This is what *metanoia*—the word used in the Greek New Testament for repentance—actually means: a change of mind. It calls for a change of thought as well as of action. It is all-embracing and ongoing.

And that is what the chapters in this first section are all about. In them we shall explore something of the spiritual reorientation that is needed if our prayer is to live beyond the desert.

# 1

# PRAYER 'IN THE PITS'

Prayer means us and God. It is the bond and interaction between the human and the divine.

Sometimes prayer can be the sweetest, most sublime and most exhilarating of experiences. Sometimes God becomes very real to us and we feel a tremendous awe or a wonderful and warm closeness to him. However at other times, and sometimes for long stretches, all this completely dries up. And prayer which used to be so refreshing now seems bitter. Whereas prayer used to feel exciting and alive, it now feels empty and dead. The ease and the inspiration, the strength and the motivation just don't seem to be there anymore.

This is prayer 'in the pits'.

People describe it in different ways. 'I'm going through a dry patch', they may say. Or they may call it a 'wilderness experience' or a 'dark night of the soul'. They may theologize and call it a 'testing time' or a period of 'purgation' or 'purification'. Alternatively they may be very straightforward and say that they are just 'cheesed off with it all'!

The commonest language used to describe this kind of experience is the image of the desert. We call it the 'desert experience'. This is a very powerful and evocative image—because the desert is a stark place, hostile and foreboding, seemingly devoid of sources of water and nutrition. The wilderness is empty and silent, dangerous and potentially deadly. This makes it a wholly appropriate analogy. It's therefore the one I shall be using most in this book.

The desert experience comes to those who pray to God. For as long as there have been people committed to following Almighty God, there has been the desert experience. If we are to survive any length of time as people of prayer, we need first of all to avoid the mistake of over-dramatizing experiences of dryness in some super-spiritual kind of way, and attaching false significance to them. People are often too quick to assume that a dry patch must mark the beginning of some torturous time of testing that God is about to put them through. People sometimes want to believe that the reason they are find-ing prayer hard is that God has decided to put them through some ordeal of purification or purgation. However, St John of the Cross (a great authority on the subject of people and prayer) has this to say: 'The origin of these aridities may not be . . . purgation, but . . . im-perfection or weakness . . . or some bad humour or bodily indisposition.' (*The Dark Night*)[1]

In other words, experience of spiritual dryness may be caused by nothing more spectacular than a bad mood or a bout of 'flu! Our mistake is to believe that our experience of prayer is magically immune to the things which shape the rest of our lives. It is as if we think that our praying will affect our lives, but not vice versa. For instance, a friend of mine once confided that he had been finding his times of prayer rather miserable of late. And he despaired because he couldn't understand why prayer should be such an un-happy experience. The fact was that his experience of prayer was on a low because he was on a low. And he was on a low because he had just ended a difficult relationship. Somehow he expected his prayer life to be unaffected by the pressures that were naturally affecting the rest of his life.


PRAYER AND LIFE

What we have to realize is that life doesn't divide into discrete compartments that are separate and independent of each other. The reality is that as a person you are an integrated whole. That is to say your mental health will be

4

affected by your physical health and vice versa; your emotional health will be affected by your social situation and vice versa; your spiritual health will be affected by your mental health, and so on. The reality is that our circumstances do have an impact on us in all these areas. And since when you pray it is you who are praying, those things which affect and influence you will inevitably affect your experience of prayer. We need to wake up to the reality that prayer and life are not magically separate.

So we can see that dryness in prayer need not be the effect of purgation or testing that God has willed upon us; it may simply be a function of where we are at, and what is going on in our lives. The feeling in prayer of emptiness, dryness or distance from God can be the product of all kinds of factors: exhaustion, sickness, moving house, a change of job, unemployment, natural body-cycles, getting married, having a baby, stress, dietary deficiency, any kind of bereavement; all these sorts of factors influence our state of being and therefore our experience of prayer. Indeed any change of life will affect us, and we may need to make an adjustment in our praying as well as in our lifestyle. That is the positive response. The negative one is to attach false meanings to our vulnerable and ever-changing moods; to tear ourselves apart trying to find some deeper 'spiritual' source of our experience of dryness, when there really isn't one to be found.

## PRAYER AND EMOTION

A second lesson we need to learn early on is to avoid the habit of assessing our prayer by our emotions. Because as we have just seen, our emotional state is dependent on a whole range of factors. Indeed our emotionality is probably one of the least constant or reliable of our faculties. Emotions certainly aren't reliable enough to be anything like an appropriate barometer for our spirituality.

Jesus told the Samaritan woman at the well that the kind of worshippers that God looks for are those who worship 'in spirit and in truth' (John 4.24). It would be wrong to take this to mean that a real prayer must be emotionally charged or prayed when we are on an emotional high. Rather, we need to be in tune with our prayer and that prayer must relate to our life as it is. That's what makes for real prayer.

Similarly there is an old adage which you may have heard in years past: 'To say your prayers is not to pray, unless you mean the words you say.' This isn't a bad saying. But again, whether or not we mean the words we say is measured not by the emotional feelings we had when we said the prayer, but by whether we are living in agreement with the prayer. Theophan the Recluse, the great mystic-bishop of nineteenth-century Russia, wrote:

> You ask yourself 'Have I prayed well today?' Do not try to find out how deep your emotions were, or how much deeper you understand things divine; ask yourself 'Am I doing God's will better than I did before?'[2]

What this means is that the quality and integrity of our prayers are indicated by how we live, not how we feel!

Knowing this can be a great relief when our emotions are on a low. Feeling emotionally empty needn't mislead us into believing that the love of God is not within us. As Metropolitan Anthony writes:

> We all know from experience that we have a variety of feelings which do not come to the fore at every moment of our lives; illness or distress can blot them from our consciousness. Even when we love deeply there are times when we are not aware of it, and yet know that love is alive in us. The same is true with regard to God; there are inner and outward causes that make it difficult at times to be aware of the fact that we believe, that we have hope, that we do love God. At such moments we must act not on the strength of what we feel, but of what we know.[3]

The truth is that if you are in Christ, then love for God is alive within you, because God himself has put it there.

> God has poured out his love into our hearts by the Holy Spirit whom he has given us. (Romans 5.5)
> You received the Spirit of sonship. And by him we cry 'Abba, Father'. (Romans 8.15)

God's gift to us of the Holy Spirit means that the cry of worship is alive within us. His grace has put prayer and love for him right within our very being. This is God's grace. Our seeming deadness is, then, only an illusory deadness. Those who are concerned about deadness are those who are alive. It is only because of the life within us that we have any sensation of our apparent deadness. Indeed we could say that the awareness of one's deadness is the most important sign of life! If your deadness or lack of love really had the upper hand, you simply would not be conscious of it. In the words of St Bernard of Clairvaux:

> Only the heart is hard that does not know it is hard. Only the heart is hardened that does not know it is hardened. When we are concerned for our coldness it is because of the yearning that God has put there. He has not rejected us.

Such a conviction enables us to have the confidence to continue to pray even when the feeling doesn't seem to be there. When we are aware only of our deadness we can still pray to God and not be rejected.


FAITH AND CONVICTION

In times of dryness, when we do bring ourselves to pray, we are in fact making a twofold act of faith. First we believe and trust in the reality and presence of God; we trust that we are in some sense before God, even though we may see or feel nothing. And secondly we believe and trust in the relationship with him that he has given us, even though it is quite invisible and intangible. We act on faith

7

in what is alive within us even though we don't at the moment feel it.

Sometimes God gives us evidence of our relationship with him: tangible experiences which reveal to us this untouchable reality. At other times he does not. These are the times when conviction and faith are of key importance in enabling prayer to stay alive and to continue. Our continuance in prayer is, then, a matter of belief and trust—a matter of conviction if not always of feeling.

It was St John the Apostle who said 'God is love' (1 John 4.16). God the Holy Trinity holds himself together with the power of love. That is the stuff of the relationship between Father, Son and Holy Spirit: the Father loves the Son and the Holy Spirit; the Son loves the Father and the Holy Spirit; the Holy Spirit loves the Father and the Son. It would be an impossible state of affairs if this were not the case! Being a Christian means being *in Christ* reconciled *with the Father* with *the Holy Spirit in us*. This means that we ourselves are caught up in the threefold divine love. This is the profound reality. This is what we are commended to believe and trust. True love for God and living prayer to God are the work of his grace within us.

In other words, at the deepest level prayer is not something which we create or which we initiate. It is not an adjunct to our lives, nor is it something which we work up. It is alive within us. Our task is to tune into the work of God, to become aware of it and to join in. Far from disrupting that process, the desert experience often comes to teach us how this task is to be done.

8

# 2

## PRAYING FRANKLY

*God sometimes 'hides himself for the very purpose that we might become real!'*

NELS F.S. FERRE[1]

Perhaps the thing that puts the biggest strain upon us in the desert experience is when we try to carry on pretending it isn't happening. We want to look as competent, as in control and as 'spiritual' (whatever that may mean) as the next person. We can find pressures put upon us, both by the people around us and by ourselves, to deny the reality of the desert in which we may find ourselves. And as long as we respond to the desert with denial and pretence, we'll be failing to meet the situation in a healthy or positive way.

### EXTERNAL PRESSURES

External pressures often have to do with other people's expectations of us, or what seem to be other people's standards. For instance, many Christians find it difficult to comprehend or allow any appearance of imperfection, struggle or suffering in the Christian life. Some reject the possibility that a Christian should experience these 'negative' things. Indeed there is much pseudo-theology about to support such an opinion. The pseudo-theology of the triumphalist is not the testimony of the universal Church and often amounts to little more than superstition.

The fact is that social, spiritual and physical suffering has always been part of the Christian experience. It is clear from Scripture that this was the experience both of Christ and of his disciples. St Paul suffered persecution, deprivation, fear and seeming failure, plus what he called his 'thorn in the flesh', which seems to refer to a permanent physical disability. Likewise his beloved disciple Timothy seems to have had constant health problems. But more than this and the testimony of the saints down the ages, Jesus himself, our Lord and our example, underwent suffering in all these forms: social, spiritual and physical. Christ in the wilderness, in Gethsemane and at Calvary shows us that God's anointed knows the suffering of temptation, struggle and exhaustion, loneliness, despair and physical agony. That was the way for Christ.

Writing to the Corinthians, Paul makes no apology that this had been his experience too. He has very little time for those whom he dubs 'super-apostles' who seem to be recommending a far more comfortable time of it!

> We are fools for Christ, but you are so wise in Christ! We are weak, but you are strong! You are honoured, we are dishonoured! To this very hour we go hungry and thirsty, we are in rags, we are brutally treated, we are homeless. We work hard with our own hands . . . Up to this moment we have become the scum of the earth, the refuse of the world . . . I urge you to imitate me . . . (1 Corinthians 4.10-12,13b,16b)

Paul was at pains to stress that suffering was authentically Christian. He concludes:

> Therefore I will boast all the more gladly about my weaknesses, so that Christ's power may rest on me. That is why, for Christ's sake, I delight in weaknesses, in insults, in hardships, in persecutions, in difficulties. For when I am weak, then I am strong. (2 Corinthians 12.10)

Likewise the writer to the Hebrews tells us bluntly, 'Suffering is part of your training' (Hebrews 12.7 JB).

Finally, Jesus Christ himself told his disciples plainly, 'In this world you will have trouble.' The theology of the triumphalist is, then, a denial of genuine Christ-likeness, and it has to do some pretty circular reasoning to avoid seeing that imperfection, struggle and suffering are inherent in the way of Christ.

Churches or individual Christians who take a rather triumphalist line tend to respond to the believer undergoing the desert experience by immediately trying to get them better, often assuming that this 'negative experience' is happening to the person because they must be doing something wrong! Indeed it is not difficult to find an army of books that take just this approach to prayer.

There are dozens of books about to show despairing believers just how far short of the mark they are falling, just how wonderful and fruitful prayer would be if they were any good at it. There are books that tell you at length of the importance and virtues of prayerfulness, and books to inspire you with all the available possibilities. The effect unfortunately is often to leave the believer feeling even more pathetic and no more able to pray than before. One wonders who such books are written for! Evidently for people with endless drive and spiritual energy; certainly not for normal people who don't have endless drive, aren't on a permanent spiritual high and who for a lot of the time find prayer difficult and dull. Such books only add to the normal Christian's sense of guilt and inadequacy and will probably do no more than aggravate the situation.

Another reason why Christians often fail to engage with someone undergoing the desert experience and give them the solidarity they need is because of a fear of the situation. People will sometimes hold back from sharing another person's suffering because they find it too challenging, too complicated, or too demanding. Alastair Campbell writes:

> Anyone who has entered into the darkness of another's pain, loss or bewilderment . . . will know the feeling of wanting to escape, of wishing they had not become involved. Caring is costly, unsettling, even distasteful at times. The valley of deep shadows in another person's life frightens us too, and we lack the courage and constancy to enter it.[2]

Because of other people's insensitivity or fear, the person going through a real desert experience can suddenly find himself in a rather lonely situation. Many churches are simply not the kind of community that can offer such intimate help. Many churches are basically not safe places in which to have major spiritual experiences—whether negative or positive! A wonderful spiritual experience may be welcomed with a puzzled 'Oh, how nice for you' sort of reaction; or a major upheaval may be greeted with a nervous 'Well I'm sure God will put it all right for you in the end'! Many of our churches—and their ministers—simply lack the breadth of spirituality to be able to handle that kind of thing. This is a sad and all too common situation.

It is in such situations and at such times that the ministry of a spiritual director is most valuable and most needed. The role of a spiritual director or 'soul friend' (to use the Celtic idiom) is essentially to help the believer to understand, perceive, interpret and respond to his or her evolving situation. Both the director and directee share in the process of learning to participate in God more freely, more fully, more authentically. The goal is to become more and more oneself in Christ, able to discern, if not understand, the movements of God. Such a process is never a private venture for the heroic lone believer. It is a process to be undergone with sisters and brothers. Sometimes God just puts us with soul friends. Sometimes it's necessary to seek out a wise spiritual director in a more formal way.

As a young Christian, I was blessed with a number of brothers and sisters in the faith, who became quite close friends. As the group grew up together, we became 'soul friends' to each other. When we reached the age of eighteen or nineteen we went our separate ways across the country to different colleges and universities. Come the vacations we all gravitated back home to share each other's

12

news, to hear of each other's joys and struggles, to evaluate what we had been doing and learning, to confess our failings to each other, and to pray together for God's continuing help. Over the years that group has dispersed and we no longer meet together in that way. But the function that the group fulfilled was a necessary one, and I have found in recent years that adopting a spiritual director is a good way of ensuring that whatever one's immediate situation, that kind of meeting, dialogue and prayer is still a regular part of everyday life.

Spiritual direction is not a crisis-solving ministry. But it is nonetheless often at times of crisis or transition that Christians first seek this ministry out. Often it is people within the monastic traditions who provide this essential ministry to the Church. In recent years this ministry has come to be more widely valued across the traditions and denominations, and it has been an important and positive development in the Church at large.

Kenneth Leech writes this:

> Spiritual Direction belongs to the desert/darkness tradition. It is sought out particularly when people are moving from security to pilgrimage, from structured forms of prayer to more inward and receptive ways of praying.[3]

In this situation, he continues, what the believer needs is not comfort or the alleviation of distress by some 'pseudo-spiritual analgesic'; rather 'they need solidarity and companionship, reassurance that they are still themselves, and, where possible, help in distinguishing the voice of God from the many conflicting voices within them.'[4]

So, in summary, pressures may come from other people or from one's immediate church environment which tempt the believer to ignore or deny the reality of the desert experience. But, equally, this denial may happen because of internal pressures.

13

These arise when we fail to perceive or refuse to admit to ourselves the discomfort of the state in which we find ourselves. The desert creates something of a tension between our belief and our actual experience. When our experience seems to contradict our belief we often refuse to admit to ourselves that this tension exists.

For instance, theologically speaking, I may be convinced that when I pray, God draws near to me, he hears me and blesses me. I may know from Scripture and from the teaching of the Church that I am bound up in an intimate relationship with God—Father, Son and Holy Spirit. I may also know from Scripture that if I lay down my burden before Christ, I will receive comfort and refreshment. But in the desert, in times of barrenness and dryness, though all this conviction may remain essentially intact, my feelings will not be telling me the same thing! My feelings will be shouting, 'God is not near, at all! I am not receiving comfort and refreshment! He is not doing anything! I can't feel or hear God at all and I do not have peace!'

For a Christian to whom doctrine is especially important, it can be very hard to own up to having such thoughts and feelings. The common approach is, 'I know these feelings aren't true, so I shall ignore them.' But ignoring them very often does not make them go away. It merely represses them into some dark nook where they can fester. People can have a lot of guilt about such feelings—indeed about any negative feelings towards God. 'I know I shouldn't be saying this . . .', they say. Or, 'I know I shouldn't be feeling this way,' or, 'No, I mustn't think it.' This way of thinking is a kind of self-torture. While self-flagellation in its literal, physical form is not a mainstream kind of activity in contemporary Christianity, Christians do it in this metaphorical kind of way all the time!

14

'I shouldn't think this way!'
'I shouldn't be angry with God!'
'I shouldn't be feeling low!'
'I've got to enjoy prayer!'

These are all lines of self-torture that modern Christians seem 'happy' to use, punishing themselves for what they are feeling.

The sense of 'doctrinal guilt' associated with feeling something that you don't ultimately believe frequently causes people to try to hide from themselves and from God what they feel when they try to pray. And such a reaction is really very unhealthy, because in effect it amounts to deliberately excluding part of ourselves from our encounter with God when we pray. It means presenting God with our heads but not our hearts. Only if we allow God to encounter us as we are—heart and mind, good and bad—are we likely to encounter much of God in our dryness.

To sum up, then, denying our negative feelings about prayer and about God will mean that we effectively withdraw part of ourselves from God. This is the very last thing we should be doing, because in this way it will be us putting a distance between ourselves and God. We need to realize straightaway that God can cope with people finding faith difficult. He has had a lot of practice! God *is able* to cope with people who are finding their spiritual journey infuriating. God *can cope* with people in pain. He *can handle* being prayed to by someone who is upset and angry because he isn't there! We do not have to treat God with kid gloves. He is stronger than that!

FORGIVING GRACE

A sense of nagging guilt makes it much harder to pray at all, let alone openly and honestly. Ironically, a sense of guilt is liable to keep a person from turning again to prayer. It's a vicious circle. One feels it would be too presumptuous to pray to God after not having prayed to him in so long! But when you think about it, to be slow to pray as a kind of penance for being slow to pray is an evident nonsense!

Does God want you to pray? The Scriptures are full of injunctions to pray, from prophets, apostles, and from the Lord himself. Well then, go on and pray! The best way of remedying the situation of having stopped praying is to start praying again, and to trust in God's forgiving grace. Lorenzo Scupoli puts it rather wonderfully in his *Spiritual Combat*, written in 1589:

> Say with great confidence in his infinite mercy: 'Do Thou O Lord according to Thy will, forgive me. Grant that I may never live apart from Thee or afar off, and that I may not offend Thee anymore.' And this done, do not spend your time in thinking whether God has forgiven you or not, because this is nothing else than pride, disquietude of mind, loss of time, and a snare of the devil, under colour of various pretexts which are good. Therefore leaving yourself freely in the tender hands of God, follow up your own practice as if you had not fallen.[5]

One of the key things this obscure Italian Theatine monk is telling us is that precisely at the moment that we return to prayer after not having prayed for some time, temptation is waiting right there to ensnare us. The temptation is to fill our prayer with endless apology for having been so long away from prayer; or to waste our time wondering whether we have been 'repentant enough' to be confident of God's forgiveness. The way to get going again, he says, is to make a succinct apology and then pray *as if you had not fallen*. The mistake is to go on apologizing in the hope that if you go on long enough you'll actually start to feel forgiven. This does not work. We would be wiser to observe Scupoli's rule. Initially you may think his approach cavalier or lax. But it is as clear as day in the *Spiritual Combat*, that the attitude to prayer which he teaches, far from being casual, is most devout and reverent. Indeed Dom de Angelis described it as a 'school of perfection for many devout souls'. To help his reader make a reverent but duly brief apology, by way of introduction to prayer, Scupoli suggests the set form:

Do Thou O Lord according to Thy will, forgive me.
Grant that I may never live apart from Thee or afar off,
And that I may not offend Thee anymore.

Alternatively you might use a liturgical prayer such as the ASB Collect for Purity as a way in:

Almighty God, to whom all hearts are open, all desires known, and from whom no secrets are hidden:
cleanse the thoughts of our hearts by the inspiration of your Holy Spirit,
that we may perfectly love you, and worthily magnify your holy name; through Christ our Lord.

Or again you might adapt the Prayer of Humble Access which sums up the picture rather well:

We do not presume to come (before you), merciful Lord, trusting in our own righteousness,
but in your manifold and great mercies.
We are not worthy so much as to gather up the crumbs under your table.
But you are the same Lord whose nature is always to have mercy.
Grant us therefore . . . so to (embrace Christ's gracious love for us) that we may evermore dwell in him and he in us.
Amen.

We must all the time remember that we are worthy to stand before God and pray to him, not because of our own righteousness but because of Christ's gracious love for us. And remember the story of the prodigal son, too. The son as he returned to the father had his little speech of humble apology prepared. It went like this:

17

Father I have sinned against heaven and before you;
I am no longer worthy to be called your son;
Treat me as one of your hired servants.

We should take note that when the young man did return to his father, speech in hand, the father did not let him finish his sorry plea. He interrupted it with an effusive welcome, treating the boy as though he were still worthy, so glad was he to have his son back with him again. And though there may be other meanings to this story that Jesus told, for me its most important message is that God is like that with us. He welcomes his children when they return to him, no matter how stumbling a speech they may have ready, and no matter how long it's been! He welcomes them back *as if they had not fallen.*

# 3

# EDUCATING THE AFFECTIONS

*A lively consciousness of mercies received . . . gives birth to gratitude.*

ST FRANCIS DE SALES[1]

Having admitted that one is indeed in the midst of a desert experience, the temptation is actually to nurture a generally gloomy, cynical or negative outlook—with regard both to God and to life in general. It's a natural tendency, but a rather unhelpful one—especially in the desert and dark times.

Such an emphasis on the gloomy is quite a common attitude. For instance, how many conversations on the streets of Great Britain begin along the lines of 'Isn't the weather awful today?' Or think of the television news: the Nine O'Clock News is always full of doom and gloom. So is the News at Ten, Seven, Six or whenever. We are usually treated to a string of depressing or worrying headlines and items, perhaps finishing off with a less serious item at the end to cheer us up. Why is it like this? It isn't the case that there is simply no good news to report. The fact is that the bad news is generally more newsworthy. It simply is not news to report that 240 jetliners landed successfully at Heathrow today. It is news to report the one that didn't. And that's quite reasonable. Unfortunately such a negative angle is often reflected in our attitude to life in general. And that's bad.

For instance, I met an old friend of mine at a conference one day. Naturally he asked me how things were going in my home parish. I was finding the work a bit hard going at the time, and I told him so. Reflecting back to me what I had said to him, he asked, 'So you don't feel you're having much success at the moment, then?' This question made me stop and think. I realized that I had indicated this. But somehow it didn't seem to be a fair assessment of the situation. Why wasn't it? I thought for a bit and remembered that in fact three remarkable and wonderful things had happened that very week. I seemed, somehow, to have just forgotten!

I learned from that conversation how easy it is to hold on to the discouragements and let go of the encouragements. Retaining a healthy outlook means letting the encouragements encourage—and not forgetting them. We need to make a positive effort to remember and share the good things rather than just focus on the negative. And this rings bells in Scripture with regard to God. In the words of the Chronicler, 'Remember the marvels he has done, his wonders, the judgements from his mouth' (1 Chronicles 16.12 JB). Similarly the psalmist writes:

> Remembering Yahweh's achievements, remembering your marvels in the past, I reflect on all that you did, I ponder on all your achievements. (Psalm 77.11–12 JB)

It is only when you put a piece of food in your mouth and chew it that you can enjoy and savour its flavour. Similarly it's only if you actually remember and keep in mind a particular encouragement that you will continue to derive enjoyment and encouragement from it. And this remembering is something which we have to do—deliberately. In following that sort of advice, we are learning to 'educate our affections'. This means through deliberate remembrance and reflection learning to appreciate and enjoy the things of God.


## GIVING THANKS

The first practical outworking of an appreciative attitude is thanksgiving: giving thanks to people and to God. Now just as when we thank people for their kindness, it isn't only when we are 'in the mood' for it that we should give thanks to God. Because not only does gratitude flow out in thanks, but giving thanks can, itself, help foster a sense of gratitude. Gratitude doesn't just happen accidentally; it can be fostered and nurtured by the healthy habit of expressing thanks, both to people and to God.

I remember talking to someone called Andrew, who had just recently become a Christian. He told me excitedly one morning how his prayer life (which itself was something of an experiment) had been transformed by adopting a new, quite simple habit, that of saying thank you to God in his prayers. He would give thanks for things which, until then, he had taken for granted that he was grateful for: food, shelter, friends, clothes, good weather—straightforward things like that. This may seem an unremarkable thing to do, but Andrew found that this new habit had profoundly affected his whole experience of prayer. And it was a joyful discovery even at a time that for him was not all sweetness and light. It was actually amid anxiety and sadness that he discovered this.

What Andrew was discovering is that we are uplifted not by being merely inanimate targets for God's blessing, as it were, but by receiving blessing with thanksgiving—taking time to enjoy what we receive from God. It's a habit that will colour our whole attitude to God. Indeed St Francis de Sales writes:

> St Thomas Aquinas tells us that the sure way of attaining to the love of God, is to *Dwell* in His Mercies; the more we *appreciate* them, the more we shall love Him . . . A lively consciousness of mercies received . . . gives birth to gratitude.[2]

## REJOICING IN SALVATION

Through the book of Psalms we can see prayers of praise and thanksgiving being kept alive even in the most awful circumstances—notably under threat of military defeat and doom. How could the psalmist, or Israel using the psalms, offer any word of praise or thanks at such times? For instance:

> How long, O Lord? Will you forget me for ever? How long will you hide your face from me? How long must I wrestle with my thoughts and every day have sorrow in my heart? How long will my enemy triumph over me? . . . But I trust in your unfailing love; my heart rejoices in your salvation. I will sing to the Lord, for he has been good to me. (Psalm 13.1,2,5,6)

The psalmist writes 'He has been good to me.' Even in the pain of what seems like being forgotten by God, the writer is recalling times past when God intervened and seemed to be very close. He recalls this not with jaded bitterness, but still valuing it. Furthermore he writes, 'My heart rejoices in your salvation.' This is important.

We must not forget our salvation. Even when being a Christian is painful and hard we need to have the sense not to take our salvation for granted. It is the greatest, most important and supreme intervention God can make in a human life. It is absolutely vital to maintain a real appreciation of that.

To that end, actually stop and ask yourself from time to time: 'What has Christ done for me?' 'What does salvation mean to me?' How will you answer? When somebody asks you, 'what has being a Christian actually done for you in your life?' what will you say?

Arm yourself for the question. Think what you will say.

Of course, we can give true theological answers about the nature of redemption, quoting deep things that are true of all who are in Christ. But we ought also to answer from the experience that is uniquely our own. When asked, say what *you* have found are the benefits of God. Say what things God has done in *your* life, what Christ has saved *you* from. Consider where you would be now were it not for God's intervention in your life. Your answer will be a unique and personal one, because God deals uniquely with each of us.

I remember being asked in a youth group many years ago, 'What has God saved you from?' This was only a matter of weeks after my own conversion, and earnestly I gave my answer. It was something that I realized God had changed for me immediately upon my conversion from atheism to Christianity. It was a personal answer from my own experience, and so I gave it with real conviction. But nobody else in the room seemed to relate to it at all! In fact they all seemed to be waiting for someone to give the *right* answer! I saw the 'correctness' of the 'right' answers when they were given, but I still believed firmly in mine. I knew what God had saved me from. It was still fresh within me, and I was very grateful for it.

What has been personal and special for you in your experience of God's salvation? These are questions on which to reflect from time to time. Making a point of remembering our salvation is the necessary first step in learning to rejoice in it.

This must surely have been in the mind of John Newton as he penned the now famous words of his wonderful hymn:

*Amazing* Grace! How *sweet* the sound,
That saved a wretch like me!
I once was lost, but now am found;
Was blind, but now I see.

'Twas grace that taught my heart to fear,
And grace my fears relieved;
How *precious* did that grace appear,
The hour I first believed!

Through many dangers, toils and snares
I have already come.
'Tis grace hath brought me safe thus far,
And grace shall lead me home.

The Lord has promised good to me.
His word my hope secures.
He will my shield and portion be
As long as life endures.

However many years it was after his own dramatic conversion that John Newton wrote those words, that sense of amazement, wonder and gratitude seems still alive, the flame still burning.

Dark times and desert times are not the time to become complacent about salvation, although it is certainly a real temptation. We can see this in the wilderness experience of the Jews:

> In the desert, the whole community grumbled against Moses and Aaron. The Israelites said to them, 'If only we had died by the Lord's hand in Egypt! There we sat round pots of meat and ate all the food we wanted, but you have brought us out into this desert to starve this entire assembly to death.' (Exodus 16.2, 3)

The Israelites were wanderers in the wilderness of the inhospitable desert, hungry and dejected, and it is not hard to see why they had become bitter about their salvation from Egypt, and entirely jaded regarding the possibilities for their future. Of course we know with the benefit of hindsight that the Lord did sustain them and give them the food and water they needed to survive. And we can see that their deliverance out of Egypt was to become one of the most crucial events in religious world history. In their darkness and dryness, the Israelites were wrongly assessing the situation.

In our times of darkness and dryness, we feel the same temptation. It is tempting to say 'I'd be happy if it weren't for God' or 'I was happy before I became a Christian.' But, rather like the Israelites in the wilderness, to say this would be to misunderstand the situation.

Appreciation of salvation has to be kept alive if we aren't to get lost and give up in the desert. Such an appreciation is not misplaced; it is an awareness of truth that will help keep us alive in the darkness of the desert journey.

# EDUCATING OUR AFFECTIONS

As we have seen, it is in part a matter of choice for us as to what we think about and what we value. Indeed it is generally those things which we think about the most that in reality we come to value the most. This is why Theophan the Recluse teaches that we should foster the 'remembrance of God' in our hearts. That way we will naturally come to value and desire him much more. We might call this 'setting our hearts upon God'.

People often say, 'Well, I want to want God more than I do,' or 'I'd love to love God more than I do,' and seem to get stuck at that point. But the fact is that what we value and what we desire is far more a matter of our own choice than we are often aware. We *are* able to 'educate our affections'. People know very well how to set their hearts upon earthly things, to have your heart set on having that hi-fi or that car, or whatever. Setting our hearts on things comes naturally to us. Let me illustrate.

## A PARABLE

Not long ago I discovered a rather special musical instrument. I decided that, all things considered, it would be good and helpful if I had one. Now initially this was just a dispassionate mental assent. But after a few weeks this mental assent had become a strong heartfelt desire, an ambition that I was now constantly aware of and I longed to be the proud owner of one of these instruments. This change was largely the result of my own efforts. I had somehow educated my affections and decided to want this object. How? The process was quite natural and second nature. I had done this:

(i)     By playing it in shops. Going into any and every shop that sold it, so that I could keep trying it out;

(ii) By staring at it and contemplating it through shop windows;

(iii) By thinking about it and imagining it in my possession; wondering what it would be like actually to own it!

(iv) By reading up on it in catalogues and magazines;

(v) By finding out about it from people 'in the know';

(vi) By telling people about it who were not 'in the know';

(vii) By constantly listening and looking out for it.

Of course you will have guessed my point. Each of these activities by which I had educated my affections has a parallel that relates to our appreciation of God. There are alternative parallels, I'm sure, but let me suggest a few. We can foster our appreciation and desire for God:

(i) By taking time to be with God. Whether we are aware of him or not, taking our stand before God in prayer, and so, in faith, coming into his presence;

(ii) By contemplating God and his goodness through visual means, using pictures, sacred art, crosses, or icons;

(iii) By thinking about God and imagining what knowing God can be like;

(iv) By learning and meditating on God and the things of God via the Scriptures and other writings;

(v) By listening to the wisdom of spiritual people and talking with fellow Christians about God and the things of God;

(vi) By sharing what we have learned with others— especially with those who don't yet know God;

(vii) By listening and looking out for the movement of God in people and in the world, for in the words of the traditional Easter greeting, 'Christ is in our midst'.

So it is as a result of our own efforts as well as the work of the Holy Spirit that the desire for and appreciation of God grows within us. In the ways I have listed above and in many others we can foster a healthy attitude to God. And this education of our affections is one way in which we can go about keeping prayer alive and warm when pressures around seem only to push the other way.

# 4

# *LOVING GOD*

*What astonishing power rests in the pure love of Jesus which is not corrupted with self-interest or self-love!*

THOMAS À KEMPIS[1]

In the last chapter we were thinking about appreciating and desiring God and God's goodness to us. In this chapter we are thinking about loving God graciously. And appreciating God or desiring God are not the same as loving God graciously.

The great spiritual writer, Richard of St Victor, wrote this in the twelfth century:

> Great is the power of love;
> Wonderful the virtue of charity.
> It has many degrees and the difference between them is great
> . . .
> Who shall worthily distinguish between them or be able to number them?[2]

Among the writers who have so attempted to distinguish between the various kinds of love and to 'number' them, are Richard of St Victor himself (!) Aelred of Rievaulx and more recently C.S. Lewis in *The Four Loves*. I'm not going to try and do that here. I want just to show something of the distinction between loving God graciously, and desiring, appreciating or hungering for God. We could call this highest kind of love by its Greek name *agapē*. Or we could call it 'altruistic' love—which is perhaps what mainly distinguishes it from the other kinds of love. For instance:

'I desire God.' Whose satisfaction is this 'I' seeking?

'I appreciate God.' Whose pleasure is this 'I' concerned with?

'I hunger for God.' Whose need is this 'I' seeking to meet?

Of course desiring God is a good and holy thing, as is appreciating God and hungering for God. But they are not in actual fact altruistic love. For instance, having a taste for Italian food, desiring and appreciating it, I might say 'I love Italian food.' This love might have an external object, but it is nonetheless an egocentric love based on how Italian food makes me feel. Desire, hunger and appreciation are kinds of love that hinge on my state of being. It's important to be aware of this difference in our relationships with people and with God.

'Gracious love' means love which is undeserved or unmerited, love which extends to anyone. Like the rain falling on both the righteous and the unrighteous it cannot discriminate. Jesus himself said:

> If you love those who love you, what credit is that to you? Even sinners love those who love them.
> And if you do good to those who do good to you, what credit is that to you? Even sinners do that.
> And if you lend to those from whom you expect repayment what credit is that to you? Even sinners lend to sinners expecting to be repaid in full.
> But love your enemies, do good to them and lend to them without expecting to get anything back.
> Then your reward will be great, and you will be sons of the Most High, because he is kind to the ungrateful and wicked. Be merciful, just as your father is merciful. (Luke 6.32–6)

Such was the example of Christ himself, who died for us while we were his enemies and prayed for his persecutors even from the cross.

If I love with this divine, gracious, altruistic, non-discriminating love called *agapē*, then the focus of that love is upon whoever I am trying to love—not on how they make me feel. With *agapē*, I love freely—without thought of merit or repayment of any kind.

It is important to understand this with regard to loving God. Because very often people confuse their love of God with the feelings that they have about God—either with the desire or lack of desire for God that they feel, or with the hunger or lack of hunger that they feel for God. It is important to know that when such feelings seem to be on a low they are not to be identified with true love for God. Feelings are not a barometer of our love for God.

But that is not to say that our love for God is beyond scrutiny.

I am simply saying that we must not assume that because the feelings aren't there that means we don't love God. We should learn to evaluate love for God on a much more reliable basis than that. We have such a basis:

> This is love for God: to obey his commands. (1 John 5.3)

> Jesus said, 'If you love me, you will keep my commandments.' (John 14.15) (RSV)

> God is love. Whoever lives in love lives in God, and God in him. (1 John 4.16)

> Where are we to look for a criterion by which to distinguish genuine communion with God from delusion? Blessed Staretz Silouan explicitly asserted that we have such a criterion—love for enemies.[3]

What these writers stress is that love for God is not some mere inward feeling. It is an empirical reality. It makes itself known concretely in our behaviour and in our treatment of those around us. This is a message which occurs again and again in the writings of St John and is echoed above by St Silouan of Mount Athos. So long as we fail to recognize this truth, then the desert experience will teach us nothing, and might even cause us to give up the Christian life altogether. It is quite possible for Christians to be living in a reality which they believe unattainable (that is, in the love of God). And because they believe it to be so, they may give up. To survive the desert experience, or any period of emotional barrenness, we mustn't make the

30

mistake of gauging our love for God by our feelings for him, because the love for God which he himself has set within us is bigger than that, and will make itself known in other ways during the dark and desert times.

## GRACIOUS PRAYER

In any case, the desert experience comes as a challenge to the nature of our love for God. Have I been loving God graciously, or has my love for him been conditional upon him doing things for me? Have I been loving God only because I expect a reward for it?

A young teacher once made an impressive wall display illustrating various ancient myths. Part of the display included a very fierce-looking and imposing minotaur. In fact, so effective was this minotaur that it was frightening the children. What happened next is fascinating. When they arrived in class in the mornings, children would go up to the minotaur and say something like, 'It's all right minotaur, you don't have to hurt me; you can have some of my packed lunch.' It is that kind of thinking that underlies so much ancient sacrificial religion; offerings are made in order to appease the god. It's an instinct that obviously runs very deep. But this understanding of worship or devotion is totally different from what should be the dynamic of Christian devotion and prayer. We pray not to appease an angry God, but in response to a loving God. Our life of prayer is our response to God's love for us—*not vice versa!*

In the words of St John, 'This is love: not that we loved God, but that he loved us and sent his Son as an atoning sacrifice for our sins. We love because he first loved us' (1 John 4.10,19). This may seem an obvious enough point on paper, but still many people tend to think of prayer only as a means of obtaining a desired response. You will even hear it said in some circles that there are only two kinds of

31

prayer: answered prayer and unanswered prayer! But this is a bad mistake.

'Lord, please do . . .' and 'Lord, please give . . .' are certainly an essential part of prayer, but they are by no means the be-all and end-all of prayer.

In his superb little book *The 60-Second Christian* Gary R. Collins pithily summarizes the journey into prayer experienced by the book's central character in his early days as a Christian:

> He had already learned that prayer sometimes involves saying thanks to God for what he is like, and for what he does. Sometimes the 60-second Christian confessed his failures and frustrations to God and asked for both forgiveness and help. At times he asked for things, and told God about his needs, desires and hopes. As the weeks went by, he discovered that he was talking to God more and more . . . He said 'give me' a lot less—and he found himself saying 'make me . . .' a lot more. He found his attitude changing so that he was less inclined to treat God like a magic genie, and more willing to ask that God's will would be done.[4]

This sums it up excellently. It reminds us that the deepest act of prayer is one of offering and self-offering, 'Lord make me . . .' And it reminds us of the temptation to operate with an experience-centred attitude to prayer. Many people do treat God like a pet genie in a bottle, and many others besides pray, if not for the experience or 'buzz' it gives them, at least expecting some 'buzz' or feeling as a matter of course. This is spiritual gluttony, and of such people St John of the Cross writes:

> They spend all their time trying to get some feeling and satisfaction rather than humbly praising and reverencing God . . . If they do not procure any sensible feeling and satisfaction, they think they have accomplished . . . nothing. As a result, they judge very poorly of God.[5]

We should be judging prayer, then, not according to the 'vibes' in our prayer times, but on the character of our whole lives. And this character will make itself known through our deeds and actions. Prayer and action belong together if either is alive. This is what St James drives home in his epistle:

> What good is it my brothers, if a man claims to have faith, but has no deeds? Can such faith save him? Suppose a brother or sister is without clothes and daily food. If one of you says to him, 'Go, I wish you well; keep warm and be well-fed,' but does nothing about his physical needs, what good is it? In the same way, faith by itself, if it is not accompanied by action, is dead. But someone will say, 'You have faith; I have deeds.' Show me your faith without deeds, and I will show you my faith by what I do. (James 2.14–18)

Faith without action is dead.

Prayer without action is dead.

Love without action is dead.

Genuine love for God, and genuine prayer, as they consist in living faith, will be accompanied by living deeds. That is the evaluation. That is the mark of a life offered to God in response to a growing unity with his divine love. This is why Thomas Merton writes these words in his *Thoughts in Solitude*: 'Actions are the doors and windows of Being. Unless we act, we have no way of knowing what we are.'

In any marriage there are times when a couple's relationship is more romantic than at other times. The couple's love for one another is not necessarily absent during the less romantic times. Gracious love, *agapē* love shows itself not through romantic sentiment but through the doors and windows of action. There is some merit in comparing the commitment made by a husband and wife to one another in the words of the marriage vows, with the kind of determined commitment the disciple should make with God.

In taking up our cross and resolving to follow Christ, we might use the words of the marriage vows as a way of

symbolizing our union with God in heart, mind, body and
soul:

> (Father, Son and Holy Spirit,
> I take you to be my God,)
> To have and to hold from this day forward,
> For better, for worse,
> For richer, for poorer,
> In sickness and in health,
> To love, cherish and obey . . .
> According to God's holy law,
> (Now and for evermore.)

The Church is often referred to as the bride of Christ, and
Christ as the bridegroom. And so the vow of the bridegroom symbolizes his commitment to us:

> I take you, N,
> (To be my friend and disciple,)
> To have and to hold from this day forward,
> For better, for worse,
> For richer, for poorer,
> In sickness and in health,
> To love, cherish and worship,
> According to God's holy law,
> (Now, and for evermore).

Christ's gracious, altruistic, *agapē* love for us is to be the
model for our love for him. Our love is not measured in
fine words or deep religious feelings, but practically, from
day to day, by living action.

# 5

# *AIMING FOR GOD*

*We mustn't be purposeless.*
*We must not exhibit purposeless-ness.*
*We must be purposeless-ness-less!*

'SIR MARCUS BROWNING MP'—ALIAS ROWAN ATKINSON,

*LIVE IN BELFAST*

Desert times and dark times force us to face important questions. As we saw in the last chapter, we find ourselves facing questions about the motives within our faith. Perhaps the key question to consider is 'What am I a Christian for?' or 'Why am I here?' or 'What is my purpose as a Christian?'

Being committed to a purpose gives stickability. When you have an overarching aim, then you have resilience. Correctly focused purpose in the Christian life will enable us to endure and survive the desert experience. Misplaced motives will be knocked for six.

Rowan Atkinson's spoof speech by 'Sir Marcus Browning MP' is a joke, a satire. It's an hilariously terrible speech. But it actually makes a good point:

> Purpose is what we're striving for;
> We mustn't be purposeless.
> We mustn't exhibit purposeless-ness.
> We must be purposeless-ness-less!
> Because we don't want to end up, do we . . .
> like the blind man in the dark room, looking for the black cat that isn't there!

If we have wandered through the Christian life rather aimlessly, then when the dark times and desert times come, we will have met our match. And lest we find ourselves like the blind man in the dark room, looking for the black cat that isn't there, we need to work out the question for ourselves, 'What am I a Christian for?' and then ask if our motivation is a resilient, durable one, strong enough to take us through the wilderness of the dark night.

It's an interesting exercise to ask Christians what they are Christians for, what they're in it for. You are likely to encounter a whole range of answers:

'Because it works!'

'Because it's fun!'

'Because it gives my life meaning.'

'Because I have no doubts as to the truth of Christianity.'

'Because it gives me a family.'

'Because it puts me in touch with something.'

'Because it gives me happiness and peace of heart.'

These are all answers that you might come across. But each of them begs a question, like 'What happens when Christianity doesn't seem to work for you?' Because such times will come. What happens when Christianity doesn't make sense of what's happening in your life? Because at some point you will find yourself in that position. What happens when you do have doubts; when you're in a cold and unwelcoming church, when God doesn't seem to be there, and you don't have peace?

Dig a little deeper and ask people what they think is the purpose of the Christian life. Again there are lots of different answers:

'To be fruitful for God.'

'To do good works.'

'To win as many souls as I can for Christ.'

'To get to know God better.'

'To manifest, actualize, and extend the kingdom of God.'

All these are possible answers. Some are better than others. All of them are part of what the Christian life is about. But none of them quite gets to the hub of the matter. What is our primary purpose then?

The Shorter Westminster Catechism of 1647 begins by addressing this precise question. It begins with a question and answer: 'What is the chief end of man?' 'Man's chief end is to glorify God and to enjoy him forever!'

I have found this to be an inspiring answer. It embraces the alternative answers because they are all parts of what glorifying God will mean. But the key distinction of the Catechism's answer is that God alone must be the linchpin of our purpose as Christians. Our purpose must be rooted in God, not in the things of God. Otherwise we shall find our faith to be quite vulnerable. If we are in it for its fruits or for conversions, we will be knocked for six when fruit and conversions cease. If we are in it for the spiritual experience, we will be knocked for six when the experience seems to run dry. The things of God are secondary to our relationship with God. We must make God himself our motivation, our joy and our strength. This is the meaning of the first question and answer in the Westminster Catechism.

## UNION WITH GOD

The Westminster Catechisms illustrate how the Puritan tradition has approached this question of the purpose of the Christian life. The Eastern Orthodox tradition comes at the question from a slightly different angle, although in the final analysis the ramifications are the same. The purpose or goal of the Christian life has been a theme central to Eastern spirituality. The words of St Seraphim of Sarov, one of the best-loved Russian saints, have been recorded on this subject. In conversation with his spiritual directee Nicholas Motovilov on a snowy winter's day in 1831, St Seraphim said this:

> The Lord has shown me that in your childhood you wanted to know the goal of the Christian life. You were told to go to church, to pray and to do good works! For that, you were told, was the aim of the Christian life. No answer satisfied you.

37

Well, prayer, fasting, and all other Christian undertakings are good in themselves. However the performing of these things is not the end of our life . . . they are only the means. The true goal of the Christian life is to acquire the Holy Spirit . . . Every work done for the love of Christ brings us the grace of the Holy Spirit. However, prayer yields it more easily because it is a weapon which is, in a manner of speaking, always in our hands . . . The power of prayer is immense, and more than any other endeavour it obtains the Holy Spirit.[1]

Since the Holy Spirit is God—God within me, as the Lord himself teaches in John 14—inasmuch as our possession of the Holy Spirit mirrors his of us, we can see that the meaning of St Seraphim's discourse is that the aim of my life as a Christian is my acquisition of God, and his of me. It is a matter of 'mutual absorption'—or, to use a more common term, union with God. (Theophan the Recluse develops this theme in his most important work *The Way of Salvation*.)

But this idea of 'union with God' isn't just some private, wonderful mountain-top experience. It embraces all our levels of being and has a practical outworking. In the words of St Seraphim to Motovilov: 'This is given, not only for you to understand, but through you, for the entire world, in order that you may be strengthened in the work of God and may be useful to others.'[2]

This truth is put rather beautifully in the teaching of Father Zachariah, another nineteenth-century Russian monk:

The aim of the Christian life consists in possessing the Holy Spirit within oneself, so that the nature of man, changed by this Spirit, as though all enlightened and strengthened, may serve its neighbours in a feat of pure love, in models of the loftiest wisdom and beauty.[3]

Union with God, or the acquisition of the Holy Spirit, is an external as well as an internal reality. Indeed it includes every level of being. The aim is union with God in consciousness and in action, or, to use a rather more biblical phrase, with all the heart, soul, mind and strength. That is to be our purpose. And it is in the context of fulfilling that, that we need to see our prayer. Prayer is not an end in itself. It is only the means—to acquisition of and by God; union with God in consciousness and action; glorifying and enjoying him, now and forever.

If we keep our sights set on this goal, then we will be able to keep our life of prayer resilient and alive.

The desert experience is always a challenge to our attitudes and motives. But this is to be welcomed. It is only if we allow this searching and purging of our inner motives to take place that the dryness and darkness will be for us an endurable, and even a positive experience.

# THE DARK NIGHT

*'What we are going to perceive today is something unknown to us'*
METROPOLITAN ANTHONY[1]

St John of the Cross is widely held to be one of the greatest mystic-saints of the Western world. Born in 1542, St John became a prominent reformer of the Carmelite Order in sixteenth-century Spain. It was he who invented the now familiar term 'the dark night of the soul' and it is he who best describes what it is all about.

In his writings St John of the Cross distinguishes between what we might call the desert experience and the experience of the dark night. The desert experience is a common experience among Christians and can refer to any prolonged period of dryness or darkness. The symptoms may include a feeling of God's absence, a feeling of emptiness and dryness, torpor and deadness. As we saw in Chapter One, these symptoms may be brought on by any number of causes. While it may feel as if God has deserted us at such times, the reality may simply be that we have an adjustment to make to our new circumstances. The feeling of God's absence is only the temporary effect our situation has had upon our feelings—not a real absence on God's part.

In contrast to the desert experience, the dark night is never an accident or misfortune. It is not the mere product of one's circumstances or situation. The dark night is always a deliberate and special work of divine grace. It is something that God does with a person for a special reason.

The words 'dark night' probably conjure up in your mind images of mental anguish or emotional torment, acute anxiety or chronic despair. But the truth is that like the desert experience, the dark night is more usually experienced as a state of dryness and deadness. Most importantly, it is characterized by the impression of God's absence. God just no longer seems to be there—not in prayer, not in worship, not anywhere.

And the dark night doesn't necessarily come to a person in times of stress and difficulty. It is just as likely (if not more likely) to come at a time of happiness, plenitude and spiritual comfort. It is quite often when everything else in life seems to be going smoothly and well, that the life of prayer suddenly goes down the chute.

This is how St John of the Cross describes what it feels like for the believer to enter into what he calls the 'dark night of the senses':

> It is at the time . . . when in their opinion the sun of divine favour is shining most brightly on them that God darkens all this light and closes the door and spring of the sweet spiritual water they were tasting . . . (Not only do) they fail to receive satisfaction and pleasure from their spiritual exercises and works, as they formerly did, but also (they) find these exercises distasteful and bitter.[2]

Archimandrite Sophrony, a contemporary mystic-saint of the Eastern (Orthodox) world, presents the phenomenon in very similar terms:

> God withdraws for a while after he has visited us. It is a strange sensation . . . When God retires there is a void inside me. He has disappeared. I am left empty and dead. When he came to me I had something that surpassed imagination. And suddenly I am back in my old condition—which before his coming had seemed normal and satisfactory. Now it appals me.[3]

In short, both writers describe how, in the dark night, all the ways in which we were accustomed to experiencing God simply cease. This is what St John of the Cross means by the 'dark night of the senses'. The language Archimandrite Sophrony uses to describe the feeling of it has a very familiar ring:

> 'There is a void inside me.'
> 'God has disappeared.'
> 'I am left empty and dead.'

But perhaps more bewilderingly than that, the believer undergoing the dark night will find continuing in his or her normal manner of prayer and worship not only difficult, but positively unpleasant and distasteful. This is a common aspect of the 'night of the senses'.

However it's important to realize that this night is only 'of the senses'. That is to say, God has not literally abandoned or deserted you: he is not really absent. What has happened is that God is no longer making his presence known to you in the same way as before. He is still there. But concealed. Note that both writers stress that it is God who has brought this about:

> *God* darkens all this light and closes the door and spring of the sweet spiritual water they were tasting . . . (St John of the Cross)

> *God* withdraws for a while. (Archimandrite Sophrony)

This bewildering experience is happening because God is at work. Indeed it is happening for a good and constructive reason.

We can call this reason 'liberation'.


## LIBERATION

In our early years as children we grow up with certain illusions. Some of these illusions are taught, others are more natural. There are the illusions that Mummy and Daddy are omnicompetent; wild animals are cuddly and fun to be with; the tooth-fairy gives money for used teeth; Father Christmas is real; God is an Englishman, and so on.

Now initially those illusions are for our comfort and benefit. They help us to cope with the big, wide world for the period of our infancy. But gradually, bit by bit, these illusions become exposed for what they are and the child is 'dis-illusioned'. Sometimes this happens easily. And sometimes not. Older children can find the transition a very embarrassing one—especially around the areas of the existence of Father Christmas and the origin of babies!

But it is adolescence that heralds a rather more dramatic process of disillusionment. And this transition is almost always an awkward one. The adolescent will question and challenge almost everything he or she has been brought up to believe, perhaps temporarily doubting or rejecting every authority—especially that of parents. It is an unsettling and painful process. But it is a necessary one if the child is to become an adult. Adolescence, perhaps more than any other time of life, is a search for authenticity and identity. It is a process we each have to go through in some way or another if we are to become truly ourselves and not merely clones of our parents or inanimate products of our society.

We can see a parallel with this in the spiritual life.

In the spiritual life the initial stage may be one of warm feelings, of certainties and simplicities, of omnicompetent leaders and absolute authorities. We grow up confident that our own brand of faith is the right one, that our church does it the right way. We are assured that if we emulate the image of sainthood or spirituality set before us, then we shall be 'kosher'. And so we learn to pray in a particular way, worship in a particular way, read the Bible in a particular way and think in particular terms. And often we become altogether too comfortable in our very particular brand of spirituality.

But at some point, we shall find ourselves uncomfortable, unfulfilled and stifled. It is as though we have overdosed on a particular medication, or run eagerly up a spiritual cul-de-sac.

Questioning—evaluation and re-evaluation—will have to happen if we are to continue in growth towards maturity. A kind of spiritual adolescence has to happen in order to help us find our true identity, to shake off mistaken or misplaced faith and learn to discern more truly between true and false, authenticity and illusion. This sort of disillusionment is a vital and positive process. It is vital that the child learns that wild animals are sometimes quite lethal. And ultimately it is just as vital to the Christian life that the believer does not persist in a faith that hasn't been thought through and that doesn't engage with life as it is.

In short we often try to put ourselves and our faith into boxes that are too small. The purpose of the dark night is to break us and our faith out of the boxes that we have built. In a whole range of ways God is wanting to break down the illusions and false expectations which we have built up around our faith. God is wanting to break us out of the limits that past experience and mistaken thinking have set on our experience of God now.

If you have found yourself shouting 'I want to be me; I want my life back!' then it is quite possible that God wants the same thing, and that it is not true faith that has stifled you, but false expectation and the pressure of illusion.


## LIBERATING GOD

It is not just illusion surrounding our perception of ourselves and our faith, that the dark night concerns. Because not only do we squeeze ourselves and our faith into boxes that are too small, we do the same with God himself.

For instance, if we become used to experiencing God in a particular way when we come to pray or worship, then we can very easily fall into the trap of identifying our particular experience with God himself or with God's presence. In other words we confuse God with our accustomed experience of God. If we do this then when we come to worship and find that our accustomed experience doesn't happen, we are liable to make the mistake of reporting that God didn't 'turn up' on this occasion. This would be a totally false reading of the situation. It is dangerously wrong to believe that because a particular sort of experience was absent, then God wasn't there. Indeed it is to make a god of something that is less than God. And that is idolatry.

When the dark night comes and our accustomed religious experience ceases, we must let it alert us to the reality that God is greater than our expectation, our experience or our perception of him. If we fail to acknowledge this, then we are in reality clinging to something that is less than God. The dark night is God breaking us out of the small world of our immediate experience and limited perceptions, in order that we may see ourselves and know God more truly. That is why St John of the Cross describes the dark night as 'the means to the knowledge of God and of self'.

That is the goal of the dark night: true knowledge and true vision.

Kenneth Leech sums it up like this:

Through this experience of darkness we come to see more clearly, we come to love more fiercely; we become more truly human. The path through darkness is in fact the way of integration.[4]

# THE WAY OF INTEGRATION

*God is the ground of all being.*

PAUL TILLICH[1]

What does it mean to live a spiritual life? Indeed what does the 'spiritual life' mean? Perhaps a mistake we make too often as Western Christians is to answer such questions in terms of certain activities that might be considered to be 'spiritual'. And so life is neatly divided into the 'spiritual bits' and 'the rest'. Perhaps the spiritual bits would include prayer, going to church, praise and worship, devotional reading, Bible study, and Christian fellowship. The other ingredients of our daily lives are necessary but less spiritual. The spiritual bits are seen as the real business of Christian living, and it is in those activities that we expect to encounter God. But this is a totally false division! It is the way of disintegration.

It is quite a common attitude amongst Christians. It is not difficult to find Christians who think of their professional lives only as a means of keeping themselves and their families housed and clothed, in order to get on with the real business of life, which consists not in secular activity, but 'Christian' or 'spiritual' activities. The Christian's professional life is compared to St Paul's tent-making. Sadly, some churches positively encourage this approach to life: sometimes directly in the teaching, sometimes indirectly, through expecting members to commit the larger proportion of their spare time to church-organized activities. This tendency within the Church to 'meeting-itis' or 'activity-itis' is, potentially, extremely damaging: to individuals, marriages, families, and to the entire ministry of the Church.

Christ spoke of his disciples as being light in the world, or his 'exhibits' or witnesses in the world, as being the salt of the earth. Fulfilling any of those callings requires that we *be* in the world. This wrong emphasis on 'spiritual activities', which so easily leads to meeting-itis, effectively sucks people into the Church, rather than sending her people into the world.

David Watson commented some years ago on this tendency:

> Christians are not to form themselves into a holy ghetto, safe from the strains and stresses of the world. The majority are to work out their high calling in Christ in the midst of a busy, competitive and unjust society ... William Temple once called Christianity 'the most materialistic of all religions' since the practical outworking of it touches every area of our daily life.[2]

Our arena for serving and meeting with God is, then, 'every area of our daily life'. To distinguish between our Christian and our secular activities, our spiritual life and the rest, is to make a totally false distinction—and one that is quite foreign to the biblical tradition. When, in the Bible, you read that in Christ God has redeemed you, note that it is *you*—i.e. the whole of your life—that has been redeemed—both the so-called spiritual and secular! Similarly, when St Paul writes, 'Your life is now hidden with Christ in God', he means *your life*—that is all of it, not just the evangelism, the worship and Bible study, but also the profession, the parenting, the social, the necessary and the mundane! In other words God has redeemed the whole of our lives, not just bits. In redeeming us he takes and sanctifies the ordinary. Our task then is to live life as a whole before God.

When we understand this, we realize that the quality of a Christian's life is to be discerned, not necessarily by the list of activities in the diary, but by the character of his or her life. We need perhaps to move away from thinking of the spiritual life as essentially doing 'Christian' things to doing all things 'Christianly'.

The way of disintegration effectively deprives God of us. Because if we go the way of unconsciously dividing our lives into spiritual and non-spiritual activities, we are in fact relegating God's lordship of our lives to certain compartments. Those are his bits. To think that way reduces Christianity to a leisure activity and God ceases to be the Lord of our lives in any true sense at all. And we cease to be his in any true sense. We have not given him 'our souls and bodies to be a living sacrifice'. Instead we have offered God bits.

Furthermore, the way of disintegration is depressing. Living a life where only the 'Christian activities' are seen as the real or spiritual or worthwhile aspect of life is a miserable way of going about things. Because ultimately it denigrates the ordinariness of life in an entirely false way, causing us to judge the majority of our time spent as time wasted. Instead we should be learning to consecrate the entirety of our lives to God—mundaneness and all—and learning to live outside our religious boxes and cliques. We will be of better service to God when we, as individuals and families, put down roots in the places where we live and get to know the people living around us. We will be of better service to God when we put down roots in our places of work and get to know the people around us there.

God is not confined to the limits of our 'spiritual compartments' or religious ghettoes. Neither should we be. As well as meeting God in the ghetto, we need to step outside it and learn to meet him there.


UBIQUITOUS GOD

The way of integration is to live our life as a whole before God. And as we have seen this will affect the character of our lifestyle. But it will also affect our expectations concerning how we are to meet with God. The way of disintegration—the compartmental approach—limits how we expect to meet with God. We pin all our hopes for encounter with God on certain activities and occasions—that special moment in worship, in our prayer time, or in a fellowship meeting. Those are the times that we expect to encounter God. It is in those activities that we make ourselves alert to discern his presence. But that alertness really shouldn't be so selective. Because God is the God of everything and everywhere. He is not confined within our activities or ghettoes. And he is free to meet with us however, whenever and wherever he may choose. Indeed the times, ways and places he does choose can sometimes surprise us.

You might pray for half an hour one evening and have no sense of God's presence, only to find that special awareness while washing the floor the next day. You might feel that you didn't really meet with God as you had hoped last night at the evening service, only to encounter his presence while doing a chore for a neighbour. God is free to meet with you any time, any place, any how: on the tube, at work, in the supermarket, in the bathroom, in the bedroom, in the pub, in contentment, in distress—even in the middle of a fight (as did Jacob!). Indeed the psalmist wrote of not being able to get away from God's presence:

Where can I go from your Spirit? Where can I flee from your presence? If I go up to the heavens you are there . . . If I rise on the wings of dawn, if I settle on the far side of the sea, even there your hand will guide me, your right hand will hold me fast. If I say, 'Surely the darkness will hide me and the light become night around me,' even the darkness will not be dark to you. (Psalm 139.7–12)

The writer finds he cannot go anywhere where he may not encounter God. Because he himself is his own meeting place with God. Wherever he finds himself, God is able to meet with him. Jesus offers this incredible privilege to all who follow him, through his promise of the Holy Spirit:

> If you love me, you will obey what I command. And I will ask the Father, and he will give you another Counsellor to be with your forever—the Spirit of truth. The world cannot accept him, because it neither sees nor knows him. But you know him for he lives with you, and will be in you. I will not leave you as orphans, I will come to you . . . On that day you will realize that I am in my Father, and you are in me, and I am in you. (John 14.15–18,20)

God has thus enabled me to know—quite irrespective of my alertness to the fact—that wherever I am, God is. And that is a truth that bears repeating: WHEREVER I AM, GOD IS! Wherever I go, I go as a meeting place between humanity and divinity! St Paul put it this way: '*You yourselves* are God's temple . . . God's Spirit lives in you!' (1 Corinthians 3.16).

This means that, in the profoundest way, wherever I go I carry God with me. And so even though I might not be aware of it, God is with me wherever I am and whatever I am doing. Whether I act accordingly or not, God enters every area of my life. Thus he potentially hallows my every moment. In the words of David Adam:

> We are encircled by (God); encompassed by his presence and his love. This is not something we create, it is a reality to become aware of; a glory that is ours but that we so often miss. We are on the very edge of glory . . .[3]

It is indeed one thing to say that we are constantly encircled by God, but it is quite another to make ourselves aware of it. Hence Metropolitan Anthony writes:

> Objectively (God) is always present, but there is some difference between being there objectively and being introduced by an act of faith into a given situation.[4]

The practice of consciously acknowledging and welcoming the presence of God into every moment and activity of life no matter how mundane, was at the very heart of Celtic spirituality. The deliberate fostering of awareness of God in everyday events was its basic element. And this was the context of the ancient Celts' use of prayer. We need to build the same awareness if we are to have a healthy and integrated vision and experience of life. We shall therefore return to the Celtic way in a later chapter.

So, in conclusion, we must understand that God is free to make himself known to us how, where, and whenever he might choose. We are not to limit him to certain activities and so put false pressure upon those activities. Neither must we limit him to preconceptions as to how he may be encountered. We must beware of fragmenting and compressing the Christian life, or of trying to tame and control God.

Without that clarity, breadth and liberation of vision our doing of prayer will always be over-pressurized, dogged with false expectation and anxiety. Our experience of prayer will be dominated by our desire for a particular kind of experience, and accompanied by the fear that that expectation might not be fulfilled. This leaves little room for manoeuvre, little freedom for God to surprise or for us to love him freely and without condition. The way of integration moves us to a place of greater love and truer vision. It is crucial if we are to survive the desert experience. It is the ultimate goal of the dark night.

# 8

# *BEING REAL*

*Whoever would enter God's ground, his inmost part, must first enter his own ground, his inmost part, for none can know God who does not first know himself.*

MEISTER ECKHART[1]

## THE ABSENCE

When we come to pray, we sometimes enjoy a special sense of God's presence, a sense that he is somehow near or at hand. But for much of the time this is not the case—the feeling just isn't there. It is often an absence rather than a presence that we experience. And our prayers can feel more like a monologue than a mutual encounter.

Obviously an encounter between two people depends on both parties for its depth and reality. In the case of our encounter with God, we have already seen that God may indeed withdraw himself deliberately from our experience (which, if protracted, is what St John of the Cross calls the 'dark night of the senses'). Sometimes God will visit us in an obvious and overt way, sometimes in a subtle and hidden way. That is God's free choice. For it is God who is responsible for God's side of the encounter. And we should be open to him presenting himself in whatever way he might choose. It has become a slogan but we must indeed let God be God!

The temptation for us is always to try and make something happen. If we fall for this our judgement of prayer becomes decidedly experience-centred and we can become subtly manipulative in the way we go about prayer. This kind of 'spiritual gluttony', says St John of the Cross, is a common temptation for 'beginners in prayer'—a category which probably includes us all! He writes:

> In receiving Communion, they spend all their time trying to get some feeling and satisfaction rather than humbly praising and reverencing God dwelling within them. And they go about this in such a way that if they do not procure any sensible feeling and satisfaction, they think they have accomplished nothing. As a result they judge very poorly of God and fail to understand that the sensory benefits are the least among those that this Sacrament bestows, for the invisible grace it gives is a greater blessing. . . . They have the same defect in their prayer, for they think that the whole matter of prayer consists in looking for sensory satisfaction and devotion. They strive to procure this by their own efforts, and tire and weary their heads and faculties. When they do not get this sensible comfort, they become very disconsolate and think they have done nothing. Because of their aim, they lose true devotion and spirit. (*The Dark Night*)[2]

In this extract John has a number of things to tell us about attitudes to prayer (he also relates it to taking Holy Communion). Perhaps the first lesson to observe is that we should not judge the reality or depth of our encounter with God by the satisfaction or other feeling that our prayer has given us. Secondly, if we spend our time trying to work up a 'sensible feeling' of encounter, then we are in fact missing the point and wasting our energies; we have lost true devotion and spirit and have started trying to twist the divine arm to accommodate our concept of prayer wrongly centred on experience. This is a mistake!

The key to 'true devotion and spirit' is to remember that God is responsible for his side of the encounter. We are responsible just for our side of it. The fact is that the absence we often feel is sometimes not God's absence at all, but our own partial absence. And the art that we need to learn is that of making ourselves present. (We shall look at this idea again in a later chapter.)

As we saw in the last chapter, the problem, so often, is that when we come to prayer, we often only bring him bits of ourselves. We ignore or shut off the less glorious parts of our lives and lift our minds to some higher plane. And some people encourage this approach when they lead others in prayer. 'Put your feelings to one side,' they say. 'In whatever mood you've come to church this morning, wherever you're at, put all that to one side. Whatever things you have on your mind—worries or concerns—put those to one side. And now we can pray!'

Now there may be a place for that sort of approach in prayer, but if I make it my general approach, what this will amount to is putting aside at least fifty per cent of my life— of me in fact—and only ever bringing half of myself to God. I will be presenting God with only the good bits of me, or the 'sound' bits—in other words the 'religious' bits of me. Consequently it will be the religious me who worships in church on a Sunday; the religious me who prays and occasionally does good works. In short it will be the religious me that I offer to God. But of course the religious me is not the real me. It only accounts for a part of myself as I really am. And in the long term this attitude will be destructive to true prayer. Metropolitan Anthony writes: 'How often prayer is false because we try to present ourselves, not as we are, but as we imagine he wants us to be.'[3]

The crucial and liberating truth to grasp is that it is actually me-as-I-am that God is wanting to meet when I pray. The incredible fact is GOD WANTS TO MEET ME! What a wonderful truth! But how rarely it sinks in.

It is because of this that we may have the freedom in prayer to be just who we are, and how we are, with no super-spiritual act, no pretence.

For much of the time we are tempted to believe that we should be feeling other than we actually are in order to pray. We think we should be feeling more spiritual or something in order for prayer to work properly. However if I decide to leave prayer until I'm feeling 'right' for it, then I shall quite possibly never pray again! Leaving prayer at the mercy of our moods like this will be a recipe for almost total prayer-less-ness. But since it is me-as-I-am whom God has loved, whom God has saved, since it is to me-as-I-am that God has come by his Spirit, the Lord will be quite able to cope with being prayed to by me-as-I-am, weak and unspiritual, imperfect and with mixed motives.

After all God does not wait until we are pure and perfect before he considers us as being 'in Christ', with all that that means. In the words of St Paul: 'God is reconciling the world to himself in Christ, not counting men's sins against them . . . so that in him we might become the righteousness of God' (2 Corinthians 5.19–21). Paul tells us that Christ died for us 'while we were still sinners'; we were reconciled to him 'when we were God's enemies' (Romans 5.8–10).

It is therefore because God has reconciled us to himself that we are able to meet him in prayer—not because of how we are or the way we feel. This means, then, that I don't have to wait until I'm feeling 'good enough' or 'spiritual enough' to pray. It means that you don't have to pretend about what state you are in when you come to pray. Are you confused? Then be confused before God! Are you happy? Then be happy before God! Are you sad? Then be sad before God! You don't have to be anything other than you are in order to pray. So don't let your confusion, your sadness or your lack of feeling keep you from praying. Come to God exactly as you are!

I am a typical Christian—a mixture of virtues and faults, good desires and bad desires, good works and bad works. That's me-as-I-am—a strange mixture, like any Christian, a saint and a sinner at the same time. In the words of St John the Apostle, 'If we say we have no sin we deceive ourselves and the truth is not in us' (1 John 1.8).

When we realize this we may be led in one of two directions: either of facing up to ourselves as we are and presenting who we are to God—as St John counsels—or of trying to run away from the darker, uglier side of ourselves, shutting parts of ourselves away and pretending that they're not there. But since we ourselves are the very place where we are to meet with God, true and deep encounter with God will require honest encounter with our real selves. This is not necessarily something that comes easily. As Metropolitan Anthony writes:

> We often turn away because we do not want to confront (our real self) face to face. Nevertheless this is the only true person there is in us. And God can save this person, however repellent he may be, because it is a true person. God cannot save the imaginary person we try to present.[4]

So we have to know ourselves if we are to encounter God face to face. If we go along fooling ourselves as to who or how we really are, then our experience of God is liable to remain sadly limited and superficial.

It is because God has reconciled himself to us-as-we-are that we are enabled to face ourselves. Because wherever we find ourselves, we will also find God. There is no part of us where God is not. This is the nature of our redemption. To be reconciled with ourselves; this has to be our attitude because our imperfection and sinfulness is not a collection of objects or forms of behaviour that we can swiftly isolate and get rid of. Our imperfection touches and colours part of us. This is not to deny the ongoing cleansing process of sanctification in which we and God are involved, but rather to say that in this process we need to 'own' every aspect of ourselves, however unpleasant, and present them all to God.

We need not be afraid to do this, because although the me-as-I-am may be unpleasant and ugly to me, it is none the less that self that God has loved and accepted, that Christ has redeemed and reconciled to God, and in whom the Holy Spirit lives and prays.

This is why we can boldly and honestly pray the ancient prayers from the Office of Compline, knowing that they reflect the heart and mind of God:

Keep me as the apple of your eye;
Hide me under the shadow of your wings.

Into your hands, O Lord, I commit my spirit;
For you have redeemed me, O Lord God of truth.

57

# 9

# *BEING IMPOLITE*

*Take your stand before God with your mind in your heart.*
THEOPHAN THE RECLUSE[1]

## POLITE PRAYER

Every Easter for some years, there has been a pilgrimage to
St Albans Cathedral. One year my youth group decided to
go along to St Albans and do some street theatre for the
benefit of those on the pilgrimage. We met on the evening
beforehand to pray. Young Richard concluded our prayers
with a prayer for the weather: 'Lord we pray for good,
warm and sunny weather for tomorrow's "open-air" . . .'
That is a nice straightforward, honest prayer, and it is at
that point that he should perhaps have stopped. Unfortunately he continued:

> But Lord if it should rain, then we would know that that was
> your will, and give you the glory. . . . And, Lord, if it's cold,
> then we will know that that's your will, too, and give you
> glory. . . . Lord, even if it should snow, we would accept that
> as your will and praise your name. . . . In fact, Lord, we pray
> that whatever the weather your will will be done . . . as we
> know it will. Amen.

Now, up until that very day it had been a glorious and hot
Easter—ideal for open-air events like ours. But the next
morning we awoke rather surprised to find snow and ice
everywhere! I remembered Richard's prayer and wondered
how many of us had really meant it—I knew I hadn't. And I
was beginning to wonder if it had been a prudent prayer!
However by noon, when we were due to begin, it had
turned into a glorious day, sunny and warm—ideal for
open-air events—with scarcely a trace of damp on the

ground. It was rather as if God had called our bluff that morning!

There was nothing terribly wrong with Richard's prayer. It had been well-motivated, it was respectful, sober, and even fairly sound, theologically. It was a most proper and polite prayer. But I would suspect that for most of us praying it, only the first sentence—'Lord, we pray for good, warm and sunny weather . . .'—was our real, honest prayer. The rest of the prayer may have been 'correct', but I don't think it was 'our prayer' in the fullest sense.

I don't know if God does ever call our bluff in regard to prayer. I think he probably does sometimes. What I certainly believe is that when we pray we should give God our real, honest prayers—even if that should sometimes seem forward, improper or impolite. If we only ever say to God what we think he would like to hear, then we are choosing to keep our relationship with him on a polite but entirely superficial level. If you are to become friends with someone, be it God or anybody else, both parties must go beyond the stage where they have to be proper and polite all the time. In a deeper relationship we have the freedom to be ourselves—as we are, and sometimes to say what is negative or difficult rather than the polite or expected thing. The desire to be real with one another takes over from the desire to be polite and proper to one another.

## TABOO

There is a taboo common to many cultures which says that one should never be the bearer of bad tidings. Some Eastern cultures take this adage very seriously. So much so that it can lead to rather infuriating situations. For instance there are parts of the world where if you ask, 'Excuse me, but is this the right bus-stop for the bus to such-and-such a place?' you will only ever be told 'Yes', because no-one will want to give you the bad news that the bus-stop you

actually need is several streets away! Not very helpful! In
the West this may seem an extraordinary custom in that it
may lead to such unnecessary dishonesty. But we ourselves frequently observe this taboo in the way we pray.
Often we don't want to 'spoil' prayer by saying the negative or wrong thing. We don't want to be too frank or
forward, and we don't want to appear impolite. And too
often this is the level at which we keep our prayers—
especially when praying in public. In doing so we reflect a
totally polite but superficial relationship with God. And I
dare say God finds it infuriating. I dare to say this because
I believe most strongly, that when I pray God wants to
meet me-as-I-am, not just the polite bits, and not a pious
act. As we saw in the last chapter, it is me-as-I-am whom
God has loved and accepted, whom Christ has redeemed
and reconciled to God, and in whom the Holy Spirit lives
and prays. God wants to penetrate beyond the superficial,
the polite and the expected, and to engage with us on a far
deeper and more genuine level. I believe he wants honest
prayer and real encounter.

## GLASNOST IN PRAYER

If you have ever been a schoolteacher or college tutor,
you will perhaps be familiar with the frustration that
sometimes results from trying to draw a class into a
genuine and spirited conversation which will honestly,
openly and rigorously grapple with the issue in question.
You are much more likely to obtain half-hearted participation with people trotting out superficial comments and
platitudes.

But the good teacher wants to know what the pupil
really thinks about the matter, and will seek to draw this
out, so that some genuine discussion can take place. And
even in a small class this can be hard to do—even with an
interesting subject to debate. One way a teacher might go

about drawing students out is to say or do something unexpected, bewildering, outrageous or provocative; something that will produce a spontaneous unconsidered reaction—whether of astonishment, bewilderment or angry disagreement. Any of these reactions are a good starting place for genuine and spirited encounter. Mr Keating in the film *Dead Poets' Society* is an excellent example of this sort of approach. Provoking people in this way, the teacher aims to break through the conventional, the superficial and the platitudinous.

Since the Lord is a God who desires to break us out of the realm of superficiality and platitude, I wonder if he sometimes resorts to this teaching method as a way of waking us up to deeper realities, and of teaching us to see and think in a different way.

Again and again in the Psalms we see the writers responding to seeming inactivity or absence on God's part. At times the psalmist is very proper and religious, saying all the things he believes God would like to hear. Sometimes it is warm and heartfelt; at others a bit idealistic or platitudinous. However elsewhere in the Psalms the writers clearly break out of any constriction to properness and politeness, or 'religiousness' and we get to see what they really think and feel about the situation. Fear, despair, anger, impatience and indignation all find their expression. The psalmist in many places gives heartfelt, frank and honest reaction to God's activity or inactivity which has provoked Israel's sense of righteous justice and indignation.

George H. Bebawi, a teacher of mine, has said more than once, 'God has three bad habits: he keeps bad company, he doesn't care about his reputation, and he's always late!' Similarly George Bernard Shaw expressed the feelings of many when he described God as an 'ever absent help in times of trouble!' Now ultimately we might not believe these things to be true about God, but at

61

times this is certainly our experience and in many places the psalmists give vent to their feelings about this situation:

Why do you hide yourself in times of trouble?

Arise LORD — wake up!

How long LORD? Will you forget me forever?

I cry out day by day but you do not answer!

Why do you sleep?

Vindicate me!

Sometimes the sense of indignation is so great in the minds of the psalmists that the prayer of their hearts—what they really feel and desire—can make very disturbing reading. Perhaps the prime example of this is Psalm 137.9, where the psalmist wants to invoke a blessing upon any who might seize the oppressors' children and dash them against the rocks. This is a gruesome and ugly text. We could hardly imagine Jesus praying such a prayer. And yet there it is within the Psalms. It is there because the psalms represent real and spirited prayer to God by ancient people brutalized in a wild and savage world. They are prayers shouted from the heart of a real people, victimized and oppressed. It is their real prayer which we read. And as such it presents the reality of the people who prayed it—both their good and their darker sides, their gentle and their savage sides. It records part of a genuine encounter between God and a real people. And that is the lesson for us: if we want our prayers to constitute a real encounter between us and God, then we must be real with him; we must present to him our real selves—both our good and our darker sides. We must acknowledge before him what we are. God cannot save the imaginary, doctored and idealized caricature of ourselves that we so often bring to him in prayer. But he will save and transform the real self which we are to present to him when we pray.

## AN EXAMPLE

I knew someone who we will call Mike. He was a Christian and an excellent jazz-guitarist. And then one day he had a bicycle accident which resulted in the loss of part of a finger. Now for anyone this would be a terrible situation. For a guitarist it is a potential tragedy. How might Mike have prayed in the middle of this? Perhaps in one or all of three ways;

> Lord, thank you for your loving care for me, which even when I can't see or feel it is still there. I praise you in this situation because I know that this accident was within your will, and believe that all things work together for the good, for those that love you. Amen.

or

> Lord, I don't know why this has happened. I want to trust you but I can't see any sense in what has happened to me. I don't understand why you had to let this happen. Help me Lord. Do something!

or

> Lord . . . You've really screwed my life up now haven't you! I'm trying to live my life for you, and this is what you do to me. Do you care? I don't think so . . .

Mike's response to the situation probably included all three types of prayer because each one of them probably represented how he was feeling about it at different times. But it is the third kind of response—the rude one—that Christians are reticent to make. They don't think it's right to be rude to God and may claim that that isn't how they feel anyway. But the fact is that we often do try to suppress or hide our anger from God. If you find the third prayer unacceptably offensive, then consider Jeremiah's complaint (Jeremiah 20.7). The Hebrew words that Jeremiah used are far more offensive than anything you'll find in an English translation!

It is because we want prayer to be all sweetness and light that we try to leave out these unpleasant and negative

63

aspects. We come to God trying to hide our anger that he so often seems to come late, to be absent or indifferent. We try to ignore our sense of confusion or bewilderment. We try to hide our indignation that he could let this happen.

If we exclude these things from our praying to God, then we are not showing God our whole selves. We are not letting him encounter us-as-we-are. Instead we are presenting him with the equivalent of a cardboard cut-out of ourselves and saying 'Here I am.'

It is a mistake to offer God only the happy and/or nice or good or religious bits of ourselves. Christ has called people to respond not in bits, but with all that is within them. Our coming to God is to be with all our heart, soul, mind and strength (Mark 12.30).

We need to be aware of where we are—emotionally, mentally, physically. Because God can only meet us where we are—he could hardly meet us anywhere else! This is why getting in touch with God so often involves getting back in touch with ourselves. Because we ourselves are the place where we meet with God.

This is part of what Theophan the Recluse means by saying that we are to take our stand before God with the mind in the heart. It means that we are to be, in the very best sense, self-conscious when we come to God. It is this consciousness that will awaken a greater awareness of our touching and being touched by God. It is this consciousness that will allow our encounter with God to continue and to deepen.

# 10

# *BEING DETACHED*

*It was in the desert . . . that the people of Israel learned the lesson of dependence upon God in the simplicity of pure faith.*

KENNETH LEECH[1]

In the last chapter we were thinking about how to respond to God when we feel wronged or when we feel grieved or angry at God's absence. But the desert experience is not always like that. People's experience of the desert is often characterized by a feeling of emptiness and torpor, rather than an experience of strong emotions. Indeed the desert is, for many, a profound experience of silence—silence from God, and silence within ourselves. God seems to have stopped speaking to us, and we seem to be left with nothing to say, nor the will to say anything.

The desert is like that. It is a wasteland where there is nothing to see or hear, just mile after mile of barren land with no relief and no scenery. It is a place where nothing seems to happen—just the sound of silence or the noise of hostile winds. There seems to be no life and nothing to see. Any life there may be is hidden deep under the ground, waiting for the rain.

This is a perfect image of the desert experience in prayer when God is nowhere to be seen or heard and we are left in a dry and lifeless state.


## SPECTATING

This calls for a radical readjustment on the part of those contemporary Christians who place an unusually strong emphasis on being able to observe God's work within oneself. Of course it is good that Christians should be concerned to see God moving in their lives. But what is often the case is that people are too concerned with watching God's work within them, rather than being satisfied to let God work within them invisibly and without their knowing. People want to be on top of what God is doing in their lives, to be able, almost, to give a 'status report' to anybody who should ask. And thus people become their own spectators—keenly following the 'show' of their relationship with God.

Now this is all very well (and indeed exciting) so long as God is working in a tangible, visible or outward way—as he does at times. But God also works at far deeper levels than the ones we can be aware of. And when God is working in hidden, invisible and unknowable ways, then the spectator finds he has nothing to watch—and his or her usual source of spiritual entertainment is missing. The relationship is still real, and God's movement is still active. It has just gone underground for a while! God's work is sometimes overt, and sometimes covert; sometimes outward and sometimes underground. Now this intermittence in the visibility of the divine hand ought not to bother us. Indeed it will not concern us just so long as our priority is to *have* God work within our lives, rather than to *watch* him at work within us. Rather than being introverted spectators we need to cultivate an attitude that is comfortable with the weaving presence of God—now visible, now hidden. We can call this attitude 'detachment' in the good sense of the word.

## SILENT GRACE

The desert is a place where God's work has gone underground for a while. Though we may see or hear nothing of God's action within us, we have to conclude that he is merely invisible for the time being and not absent. Having an attitude of detachment will save us from unnecessary despondency in the desert. Detachment will free us to be comfortable with silence and gives God the freedom to work in silence. I have a story which illustrates this principle.

## ALLOWING SILENCE

A number of years ago I travelled as part of a small team to visit a church in East Anglia. We had been invited to lead a 'renewal' weekend. The first evening meeting came and went in the usual sort of way for these events. The second of our evening meetings came and we expected an order similar to that of the previous evening: songs of worship—prayers—teaching—silent waiting upon God—prayer with laying on of hands. However when we came to the silent waiting, what followed was silence, more silence and yet more silence! In fact it continued for about half an hour. For those of us leading, this was quite bewildering. This silence was not the mere absence of noise, it was something very profound. It was almost tangible, and people were extraordinarily still. I wanted to know what was going on, what God was doing. But the only answer I had to my question was a strong sense that the Lord wanted us to remain still before him. So we did. There was no outward sign of God working within people other than the silence itself. Eventually we drew the meeting to a close with some songs of worship.

Now we were not aware of anything having happened. As far as we could see, nothing had happened. But over the next day or so, a number of people came to the team's leader to tell of how, in various ways, they had met with God that evening. Perhaps the most dramatic report was of a lady who had been healed of a long-standing emotional problem. In the total silence God had delivered her. A deep healing had happened within her, silently and invisibly, but quite definitely! It was a quite extraordinary experience. The point is that while we had been leading the meeting, nothing other than the silence seemed to be going on. As we spectated, we could see nothing. It was only after the event that we learnt of God's work among us.

The Christian life is often like this. It is often at the times when God seems to become quiet and distant that he is in fact doing the most profound things. At the time, though, we only sense the absence of anything happening. Much later, with hindsight, we may discern that this seeming absence concealed a profound work of grace within us. You may well know this short meditation but I quote it because it speaks rather beautifully of this truth:

> One night a man had a dream. He dreamed he was walking along the beach with the Lord. Across the sky flashed scenes from his life. For each scene he noticed two sets of footprints in the sand. One belonged to him and the other to the Lord. When the last scene of his life flashed before him, he looked back at the footprints in the sand. He noticed that many times along the path of his life there was only one set of footprints. He also noticed that it happened at the very lowest and saddest times in his life. This really bothered him and he questioned the Lord about it. 'Lord, you said that once I decided to follow you, you would walk with me all the way. But I have noticed that during the most troublesome times in my life, there is only one set of footprints. I do not understand why, when I needed you most you would leave me.' The Lord replied, 'My precious, precious child! I love you and would never leave you. During your times of trial and suffering, when you see only one set of footprints, it was then that I carried you.' (Anon)

One day all will be made clear. In the meantime it is very much a question of faith. It is relatively easy to trust in God when divine interventions seem to be commonplace. It is far harder to trust God when he seems impossible to find. It is easy to believe that the Lord is your shepherd when you lack nothing and enjoy fullness and refreshment.

It is far harder to believe it when you find yourself in the valley of the shadow of death. The light of hindsight may show us these mysteries. In the meantime we follow in the darkness of faith.

In the darkness of this faith we might pray the following words of Thomas Merton as he reflected on a similar thought:

> My hope is in what the eye of man has never seen; Therefore let me not trust in visible rewards.
>
> My hope is in what the heart of man cannot feel; Therefore let me not trust in the feelings of my heart.
>
> My hope is in what the hand of man has never touched. Do not let me trust what I can grasp between my fingers. Death will loosen my grasp and my vain hope will be gone.[2]

Sometimes the divine presence is very real and very obvious. At other times he is veiled or hidden. But he is always there. The divine presence is constant—sometimes overt and sometimes covert. This is the God in whom we try to trust. This is his weaving presence. Detachment, of the sort we described earlier, will help us to live with our God and not be too disturbed by his mysterious ways!

# PART 2

*Finally, grow strong in the Lord, with the strength of his power. Put God's armour on so as to be able to resist the devil's tactics. For it is not against human enemies that we have to struggle, but against the Sovereignties and the Powers who originate the darkness in this world, the spiritual army of evil in the heavens. That is why you must rely on God's armour, or you will not be able to put up any resistance when the worst happens, or have enough resources to hold your ground.*

EPHESIANS 6.10–13 JB

# Introduction

In the letter to the Ephesians this text is followed by a quick course in spiritual self-defence, the overriding concern being that the Christian should be able to stand his or her ground, come what may. A lot can be made of the imagery of the various bits of the 'armour of God', indeed rather too much at times, I suspect. We mustn't lose sight of the basic point, which is that truth, righteousness, preparation, faith, salvation and the word of God all enable us to hold our ground when the going gets tough. This list is immediately succeeded by a command to pray:

> Pray in the Spirit on all occasions and with all kinds of prayers and requests. With this in mind be alert and always keep on praying for all the saints. (6.18)

Our resistance when the worst happens will depend heavily upon both our perseverance in prayer and our ability to use all kinds of prayers. Just as our physical health weakens and fails if we eat only one type of food, so our spiritual health will deteriorate if we use only one type of prayer. Prayer often becomes unpalatable and boring because we have overdosed, so to speak, on one kind!

In Part Two we shall be thinking about different kinds of prayer. We shall take a look at some exercises, or forms of prayer, which can still work in a spiritual desert and bring sustenance in times of darkness and dryness. Each aims to bring a different consciousness into our experience of prayer, a consciousness which will begin to enable us to find God again when he seems to have all but disappeared.

# 11

# *BEING STILL*

*It is better to keep quiet and be, than to be fluent and not be.*
ST IGNATIUS OF ANTIOCH

For the average twentieth-century Westerner, being still does not come easily. We are too used to being constantly active and constantly bombarded with noise. We become so accustomed to the distraction of this permanent bustle that stillness can feel quite uncomfortable. Being still before God may initially seem an uncomfortable thing too. Because it means coming to God without anything between him and you—not even words. Words often serve as something to put between him and us, and can sometimes become a barrier rather than a help. Coming to God with words can sometimes hinder us from meeting with him more directly. This happens with people too.

Maybe at parties you have had the experience of being introduced to someone who then hijacks you, talking at you nineteen to the dozen, asking you questions, and rabbiting on before you can answer. And there you are, trapped in a corner, looking for a way of escape. Having extricated yourself from the awkward situation, you will be aware that you didn't actually meet that person, you simply encountered words. What the person had been communicating—intentionally or not—was 'Don't meet me, meet my words!'

Sometimes this is what we do with God.

I remember leading a service in a church in south Devon. After a time of singing I said, 'Let's now be still for a while. Let us be silent in God's presence.' The people were silent. But only for a matter of seconds before a man at the back decided that he just had to pray something aloud! 'Let's be *completely* still now,' I said. A few more seconds elapsed before another person felt they just had to pray something aloud! It was becoming clear that these people just weren't going to comply. They couldn't cope with the silence. It was another case of 'Don't meet me, Lord; meet my words,' but on a congregational level!

Coming to God in silence lets another barrier down—there are no words to hide behind. It's like coming to God naked. And this can feel uncomfortable. However, learning to be silent with God is crucial if we want our encounter with God to become deeper and more direct.

A couple of years ago I took a long summer vacation at my home in Bath. Over the course of the summer months I had some fifteen or so different people come to visit (Bath is a beautiful city!). On reflection, I realized that the guest whose company I had found most real and refreshing was the guest with whom I had spoken the least. We had spent a lot of time just reading quietly to ourselves—not even communicating with each other. Now there are two ways I might describe that encounter. I could say, 'I had a friend to stay last weekend, and she hardly spoke to me. Why, one afternoon she had her head buried in a book; scarcely a word of conversation!' That way I have made the silence seem a negative experience and the listener concludes that something must have been wrong for this silence to have occurred. However the truth of it was that we were both quite comfortable being silent together—because we knew each other well. We didn't feel we had to be constantly chattering in order to enjoy each other's company. Similarly silence is the place where our relationship with God can become deeper. The ability to pray well and from the heart—rather than bombard the Lord with words—stems from the ability to be still before God. A practice of silence will improve our practice of spoken prayer.

The stillness we need if we are to rediscover prayer is not just an absence of noise or words: it is an inner stillness. An inner stillness means an absence of hurry. It has often been said that hurry is the arch-enemy of prayer. The speed and busyness of modern-day life can make it hard for us to pray in a quiet and unhurried way—but there are ways and means.

Carl Jung tells the story of a man who was seeing him for therapy. When trying to book the next session, Jung's client was most insistent on wanting a particular time on a particular day. 'I'm sorry,' said Jung, 'but I already have an appointment booked then.' And so, rather put out, his client settled for an alternative day and time for his appointment. When they next met, the client was indignant. 'You told me that that appointment was taken,' he said angrily. 'And yet on that very day at that precise time, I saw you! You were sitting on the bank of the river doing nothing but dangling your feet in the water!' 'That's right,' admitted Jung. 'That was the appointment. It was my appointment with myself—and I never break it!'

Each of us needs to keep such a discipline if we are to catch up with ourselves and be still with God. The pressure of modern-day living is such that we rarely take time to be where we are; we are always living in the next moment, doing what we are doing but with half a mind on what we have to do next. Being still means actually being where we are for a while. It requires that we take some time out to stop chasing our tails for a moment and catch up with ourselves—ourselves being our meeting place with God. If we will not take time regularly to slow down and catch up with ourselves, we should not be surprised if we seem to be out of touch with God.

Jung's habit of writing into his diary a sacrosanct appointment with himself is one which we could all benefit from. Making a sacrosanct appointment is a key preliminary to meeting with God in the fullest way.

## BECOMING STILL

Ideally our appointment with God should be relaxed but not sleepy. It should be alert but not tense. We should be conscious of ourselves, but not busy thinking. The Church Fathers called this the state of being 'recollected'. It is the state of attention and awareness which comes from having 'collected ourselves' and become quieter. It is a state of undivided consciousness.

In order to achieve this, we need to acquire a degree of self-control. Mental and physical fidgeting have in some way to be checked.

Physical fidgeting is relatively easy to deal with. It's not a case of eradicating all physical movement, but just of being comfortable. So practise finding a comfortable posture for prayer. You might favour a particular chair, or a back-stool. If you can make yourself physically comfortable, then you will have removed a common cause for distraction or sense of hurry in what you are doing.

Mental stillness generally takes more practice. Firstly you should be aware that in turning aside from the usual rush and bustle you will, by removing the distraction, become more acutely aware of how you are feeling. It is when you leave off and stop that you realize how tired you are. Becoming still will bring you back in touch with your tiredness, your excitement, your sadness, your worry, or whatever it is. In the stillness you will start to become aware of how you are. It's good to be aware that this will happen and so not be too disturbed by these things surfacing. The thing is to be aware of what you're feeling rather than distracted by it.

Another thing that you are likely to find when trying to be still is that as soon as you are comfortable and quiet you will suddenly start remembering a hundred and one things that you have to do: the phone call that needs making, the letter to write, the item you have to buy, the bill you have to pay, etc. All these things intrude, clamouring for attention, and so we spend the time we should spend being still, thinking 'Now I mustn't forget that.' And immediately we are distracted. With practice it is possible simply to brush these thoughts aside for the duration of your quiet. They might be subjects for your prayers later on, but for the moment they will serve only as an impediment to becoming still.

An initial help is simply to use a notepad. If something does come to mind that you are anxious not to forget, rather than trying to hold it at the back of your mind while you try to be still and concentrate, it is better to note it down. Write it down and keep the notepad just outside your line of vision. That done, you will be able confidently to put the matter out of your mind for the time being, and to maintain a state of outward and inward quiet.

In the longer run, the problem of what the Fathers termed 'intrusive thoughts' can be more swiftly dealt with: just mentally pushing them aside. It takes some practice to be able to concentrate that way, but it does come. In the meantime the notepad is a useful help.

Becoming concentrated and 'recollected' is vital if prayer is to become deeper and more potent. And there are ways of attaining recollection which in the long run are far more signficant and far-reaching. 'Bridging Work', 'Bridging Noise' and the 'Prayer of Attention' serve as a way in to the silent communion with God that lies at the heart of all prayer—verbal or not. We shall be looking at each of these in the following chapters.

# 12

# *BRIDGING WORK*

*Our sanctification does not depend upon changing our works,
but in doing that for God's sake, which we commonly do for our
own.*

BROTHER LAWRENCE[1]

The practice of bridging work aims at two things; firstly it
uses work or activity which by allowing movement helps us
to cope with outward silence; secondly it aims at making
us aware of ourselves—the place where we meet with
God—and fosters a deep inner silence. In short it is a
bridge to the state of recollection which we talked
about in the last chapter. It is a form of prayer which
makes us more fully conscious, more aware of ourselves
and our surroundings, and potentially more conscious of
the presence of God, which is always there, if not always
perceived.

Metropolitan Anthony tells us a story about knitting as
bridging work. An old lady once came to him, when he was
a young priest, to ask for some advice concerning prayer.
'These fourteen years,' she explained, 'I have been praying
the Jesus Prayer almost continually, and never have I perceived God's presence at all!' Metropolitan Anthony's
reply was this:

> If you speak all the time, you don't give God a chance to (get)
> a word in! Go to your room, put it right, put your chair in a
> strategic position . . . and first of all take stock of your room.
> Just sit, look round and try to see where you live, because I am
> sure that if you have prayed all these fourteen years it is a long
> time since you have seen your room. And then take your
> knitting, and for fifteen minutes knit before the face of God.
> But I forbid you one word of prayer! You just knit and try to
> enjoy the peace of your room.[2]

The result of following this advice was, for this lady, the most wonderful and profound experience of a silent encounter with God. The knitting was just a help, a bridge to the stillness in which she met with God.

I must stress that bridging work is not something which we do in order to make God reveal himself to us. The effect is upon ourselves. It is a way of making us conscious of the constant reality of God's presence. David Adam puts it this way:

> The history of salvation and incarnation has to become our own personal history. The Celtic way of ever inviting God into their activities, and seeking to become aware of him in everyday events, is the natural way of achieving this. . . . We are encircled by (God); encompassed by his presence and love. This is not something we create, it is a reality to become aware of, a glory that is ours but that we often miss.[3]

Bridging work is a way of tuning into that glory and making that awareness our own. As a spiritual exercise it is an extremely accessible and potent one—especially for those of us with hectic schedules. Many of us live in a terrible rush these days. And Christians who live at the modern rate often think that all they can manage is to grab a few hurried moments of prayer here and there—snatching prayer like they might snatch a faster than instant max-pak coffee. Bridging work is a particularly user-friendly spiritual exercise for such people because it does not require the adding of yet another activity to their already badly overloaded timetable. Instead it involves doing certain activities already timetabled, although somewhat differently.

TAKE A RISK

The simple way to begin is to take a task. Choose a mundane, practical chore that you would have to do anyway—

preferably a manual, non-cerebral sort of activity: washing-up, cleaning a bicycle, washing a car, weeding, raking, dusting, polishing—anything like that.

The next thing is to decide to do it. I say that because the usual way of doing chores is to do them with half one's mind on something else; we might for instance wash the car while listening to the radio, or do the ironing while half watching the television. In other words we usually do chores with only half our attention. To use a chore as bridging work, you must make a deliberate decision to do the chore and that alone. It might help to say out loud to yourself, 'I am now going to wash the car before the face of God,' or whatever. And then do the task but with all your attention instead of the usual half. Do it slowly, carefully and in silence. It doesn't matter that there will be noise and movement around you, just do it silently and calmly. As you work, concentrate on the physical feeling of what you're doing—the sensation in your hands, arms, legs, feet, body, neck and head. Become aware of the smells and sounds around you as you work. Gradually you will find your silence becoming an inner stillness, a state of peace in which you will be more aware of God's encircling presence. By making you more conscious of your surroundings and more conscious of yourself, bridging work makes you more wholly conscious altogether. It brings you back in touch with yourself and your body which is the very temple of God's presence, as St Paul tells us. Thus it is a bridge to recollection—the state where we are most receptive to God—the state of undivided consciousness.

Bridging work, then, isn't about doing a spiritual activity, it's about doing an ordinary activity differently. In the words of the song: "T'aint what you do; it's the way that you do it!' It's a matter of sanctifying the ordinary. That's what Christ did by becoming incarnate.

# 13

## *BRIDGING NOISE*

*Shut-up—but gradually!*

Just like bridging work, bridging noise is a bridge from our usual state of distractedness and disintegration to a place of integration and inner quiet, the state of being re-collected. It is a way of enabling us to shut up gradually.

Let me suggest four types of bridging noise:

(i)  Environment
(ii)  Music
(iii)  Meditation
(iv)  The Prayer of Attention

We shall focus on the prayer of attention in the next chapter. In this chapter we shall consider the first three.

### ENVIRONMENT

Using the environment as bridging noise is a very similar exercise to that of bridging work. It is an exercise which can be done while walking or while sitting still. It simply involves beginning your 'appointment' by hearing and listening.

Don't strain to hear things. Just be relaxed and become aware of the noises that are around you.

For instance as I sit here I can hear the noise of traffic on the road, the sound of the wind in the trees, the breeze rustling my papers on the desk, the distant rush of the motorway, doors opening and closing, the singing of birds, the whirring of my typewriter, the intermittent shunting noises of trains in the distance, the occasional rumbling of my stomach, the sound of me swallowing. . . .

Even though not all the noises will be restful or natural

ones, becoming aware of them will gradually bring about a certain stillness and peacefulness within you—a state that then enables prayer, whether spoken or silent, to be much deeper and more conscious.

## MUSIC

Music is remarkably powerful. It is able to affect our bodies, minds and emotions; it uplifts, invigorates, quietens and relaxes us. Indeed people everywhere use music as a bridge all the time.

Many people when they get home from work in the evening will immediately turn on the hi-fi and 'mellow out' to their favourite album. In doing that they are using music as a bridge from a state of tension and agitation, to one of quiet relaxation.

We can use music similarly as a preparation for prayer. Tastes vary of course, but for helping me to become still, I have found particular music to work especially well: that of Thomas Tallis, Peretinus, or Palestrina (which is medieval heavenly-sounding stuff) as well as more modern music such as the song 'Where do we go from here?' as sung by Chris Eaton. Non-vocal music is often even better. The gentle guitar work of the Franciscan monk John Michael Talbot has become popular in recent years for exactly this type of use. Indeed one of his albums is entitled *Come to the Quiet*. Such music is not just music for its own sake, but stills the heart and mind from the noise and hurry of everyday living in the modern world. It is meant as a bridge to silence and, as such, a prelude to encounter with God.

In recent years, particularly among churches involved in the charismatic renewal, there has been an encouraging increase in the sensitive and generous use of silence within corporate worship. And many songs or choruses have been written which are designed quite deliberately as a bridge from noise to silence. In particular the early songs from the

Vineyard Fellowships in the United States were written in such a way that they lend themselves to this use as bridging noise.

Similarly, from the Catholic end of things, the beautiful music of Taizé has come to be widely used and loved. In simple but beautiful harmony the chants work as short repeated phrases of prayer, vehicles for the silent prayer of the heart. Their singing and repetition brings people in touch with the silent, inward prayer of their hearts in an unusually effective way. Thus they are achieving what Theophan the Recluse referred to as standing before God with the mind in the heart. I think that's a marvellous phrase because it expresses so well the state of undivided consciousness that 'recollection' means.

Modern technology enables us to benefit from this sort of choral music even in our private devotions as an aid to recollection—and so to prayer.

## MEDITATION

Meditation is a vast word that can mean many different things even within the Christian context. It includes what the Church has called *lectio divina*. This means the slow and attentive reading aloud of Holy Scripture or some other writing such as one of the Church Fathers. It can also include reading sacred poems aloud as a way of wrapping one's mind round a subject or idea. The use of sacred poetry has been very much a part of the tradition of Christianity in the British Isles since the very earliest Celtic Christians.

But at its simplest, the word 'meditation' simply means thinking. The key differences between normal minute-to-minute thinking and that which we might consider to be meditation are these:

(a) meditation is coherent thought;
(b) it has a chosen subject;

(c) it has a purpose: the apprehension and appreciation of a truth—hence the use of sacred literature.

## User-friendly Meditation

In its simplest form, meditation as 'focused thinking' is a useful and highly portable spiritual exercise. For instance, a few years ago a young friend of mine called Dean, then about six years old, was out shopping with his mum. When they came to the supermarket check-out there were long queues. And the people queuing were, not surprisingly, impatient. They waited for about half an hour. And all the time they were waiting there was a man behind Dean and his mum who was proving a great irritation to his neighbours by incessantly rambling on about the queues and how it was absolutely typical and how the people on the tills didn't know what they were doing and how awful the prices were and how the country was going to the dogs and it was all the government's fault, and so on. Eventually, ignoring his mother's repeated dissuasions, Dean turned round to the gentleman and said:

'Do you believe in God?'

'Well, as a matter of fact, I do,' said the man.

'Well, why don't you think about him instead of about the queue, then?'

The man amicably roared with laughter—which was a relief to all! Dean's mum took up this advice by quietly singing a hymn to herself as she waited. It was good advice, because we can exercise choice as to what we think about. There are many times in the day when we have time to think: taking a walk, standing on the train, sitting on the bus, lying in bed. Make a deliberate choice as to what you will think about. Indeed St Paul, writing to the Philippians, says:

Whatever is true, whatever is noble, whatever is right, whatever is pure, whatever is lovely, whatever is admirable—if anything is excellent or praiseworthy—think about such things. (Philippians 4.8)

*'Don't think, look!' (Ludwig Wittgenstein)*

In the first church I attended, the assistant minister, a certain Barry Kissell, was a source of great inspiration to me, and a fine example in my early days as a Christian. His sermons always fascinated me. From time to time he would relate some commonplace activity he had been doing during the week and describe something he had seen or heard. Then he would say, 'And you know, that reminded me of God!' or 'And I thought to myself, "Well, God's like that, isn't he?"'

At the time it seemed that this was just an amusing way of making an illustration. But I see now that it may well reflect a certain spirituality or 'awakeness'. Because it seems to me that such sayings indicate a man who goes about everyday tasks—at least some of the time—with his eyes and ears open, using his senses to make himself aware of God and to develop his appreciation of God. Adopting such an attitude turns the whole of one's environment into an object for contemplation, the whole of creation into a text for meditation. And meditation can be a bridge to prayer. What Christian, for example, could stand before a great landscape, seascape or mountainscape and not be aware of the greatness of God? What Christian could take in the sight and not feel the stirrings of a prayer rising up to God? In such places even the least 'spiritual' person finds creation an object of meditation, and that meditation a bridge to prayer. As the psalmist wrote, 'The heavens declare the glory of God; the skies proclaim the work of his hands . . . (Psalm 19.1).

*Lectio divina*

We have so far considered meditation in its most 'portable' mental forms. Such meditation can affect our inward state

86

as we go about our daily business. *Lectio divina* is a form which we can use in a more formal time of prayer.

Start by choosing a text—a passage from Scripture, a sacred poem, a piece of liturgy, or a passage from one of the Church Fathers. And then read it aloud. Read it soberly, attentively and seriously—that is without trying to create a feeling or an atmosphere, concentrating on the meaning of the words with fullest attention.

The anonymous pilgrim who narrates his story in *The Way of a Pilgrim*—apparently the journal of a Russian pilgrim written in the 1850s—writes of visiting a church where the young priest 'celebrated very slowly indeed, but with great devotion'. One of the parishioners had warned the pilgrim on his way to the church, 'Don't hurry, you'll have plenty of time for standing about when the service begins. Services take a long while here; our priest is in bad health and goes very slowly!' The pilgrim goes on to describe his meal with the priest after the service:

> During the meal I said, 'How reverently and slowly you celebrate, Father!'
> 'Yes,' he answered, 'but my parishioners do not like it and they grumble. Still there's nothing to be done about it. I like to meditate on each prayer and rejoice in it before I say it aloud. Without the interior appreciation and feeling, every word uttered is useless, both to myself and to others. Everything centres in the interior life and in attentive prayer. Yet how few concern themselves with the interior life,' he went on. 'It is because they feel no desire to cherish the spiritual, inward light.' 'And how is one to reach that?' I asked. 'It would seem very difficult.' 'Not at all,' was the reply. 'To attain spiritual enlightenment and become a man of recollected interior life you should take some text or other of Holy Scripture and for as long a period as possible, concentrate on that alone all your power of attention and meditation; then the light of understanding will be revealed to you.'[1]

The attentive oral repetition of a text in this way aims at a greater apprehension and appreciation of a truth. The by-product of this concentration is recollection—the place of silent communion with God.

It is a good practice to use a meditation such as the opening to Morning or Evening Prayer or the text below from David Adam's collection of prayers in the Celtic tradition. Their slow and thoughtful recitation helps us to form an awareness of the miracle in which we stand, the very presence of God:

> We have come together as the family of God. . . . in our Father's presence . . . to offer him praise and thanksgiving . . . to hear and receive his holy word . . . to bring before him the needs of the world . . . and to seek his grace . . . that through his Son, Jesus Christ, we may give ourselves . . . to his service.'[2]
>
> I weave a silence on to my lips
> I weave a silence into my mind
> I weave a silence within my heart
> I close my ears to distractions
> I close my eyes to attractions
> I close my heart to temptations
>
> Calm me, O Lord, as you stilled the storm.
> Still me, O Lord, and keep me from harm.
> Let all the tumult within me cease.
> Enfold me, Lord, in your peace.[3]

# 14

# *THE PRAYER OF ATTENTION*

*How can you expect to be heard by God, when you do not hear yourself?*

ST CYPRIAN

The desert experience is always disruptive to prayer. Whatever the forms or pattern of prayer you have become accustomed to using, the desert or the dark night will make it very difficult to continue praying in quite the same way. Indeed, the desert experience is a challenge to any form of prayer.

Having said that, however, the ability to use 'all kinds of prayers' will be of great advantage in enabling the pilgrim in prayer to adjust to the new and hostile circumstances of the desert experience. Expanding our repertoire in prayer is always a good and healthy practice and one which will stand us in good stead when the going gets a bit tough.

It is therefore much to the Christian's advantage to explore different practices of prayer; to ask Christians of other denominations and traditions how they go about prayer, and to see if we mightn't profit by the same practices. (Any rapprochement of traditions which encourages this kind of honest exploration is in my view, therefore, a good thing.)

## FORMS OF PRAYER

There are of course many and various kinds of prayer. But to be crude and simplistic for a moment, let's imagine that they divide roughly into three categories: silent, set and spontaneous.

Silent—Pretty obviously, this type of prayer is not spoken. It may include prayers 'spoken in the mind' or it may not contain any verbal element at all. It may include physical expressions of prayer such as kneeling, raising hands, making a sign of the cross, or of the kind we explored in the chapter on 'bridging work'.

It is a category of prayer central to the contemplative traditions and is developed in different ways by writers such as Brother Lawrence in the West and Gregory Palamas in the East.

Set—This is where the words of prayer are pre-selected or prescribed. It is then the job of the worshipper to turn those words into prayer. It is the earliest authenticated traditional Christian approach to corporate prayer and worship. The Church's body of set or prescribed prayers is what the word 'liturgy' (which originally just meant 'the work of the people') has come to mean here in the West. This way of prayer has been most thoroughly developed in the Catholic, Anglican and Orthodox Churches.

Spontaneous—Obviously, this is the type of prayer that you make up as you go along (not that that should imply any the less effort behind it). It is the model of prayer most commonly used in charismatic and Free Church traditions—sometimes led and sometimes 'open' or shared. For many it is the most natural kind of prayer, approximating, as it does, to the way we talk to family and friends.

In this chapter we shall be concentrating on the Prayer of Attention, which is a way of going about the set kind of prayer.


FORM AND ESSENCE

But before we do, we must put these various forms of prayer into their proper perspective. And that is to remember that the prayer does not equal the form. The prayer is always more than the words or the silence used. The form is just the visible tip of the iceberg, so to speak. It is the audible or visible expression of what is silent and invisible—the interior prayer of the heart or of the mind. We often become too concerned with the outward form— which is secondary—and neglect the interior dimension which is what actually makes a prayer a true and living prayer. In the words of Metropolitan Anthony:

> One of the reasons why communal worship or private prayer seems to be so dead or so conventional, is that the act of worship which takes place in the heart communing with God is too often missing. Every expression, either verbal or in action, may help, but they are only expressions of what is essential.[1]

So it is the interior element that is essential. Without it the outward form will be empty and useless. It will not be living prayer. It will indeed be 'dead and conventional'— not to say dead boring!

The outward form, whether verbal or in action, is only an expression or a help. The interior prayer is what is primary. Sometimes the worshipper will be able to express this interior prayer in words, and sometimes not.

Some years ago I was a member of a youth group called 'Ichthyans'. Corporate spontaneous prayer was always a part of our worship together. My friend Jonny was an eager and earnest participant in these times of 'open prayer'. You only had to look at him or to listen to the sound of his voice to know that when he prayed, he was praying from the heart. But he would frequently become tongue-tied in his prayers, and finished a good many of them rather frustratedly with the words 'O Lord . . . you know what I mean!'

And this made perfect sense. There was clearly a prayer going on there. Jonny just hadn't quite managed to express it. It is reassuring to know that when you pray, as Selwyn Hughes says, 'God hears you, not merely what you say!'. So while Jonny hadn't quite found all the words he needed, God, who sees the heart and knows our thoughts and desires even before we ask, knew just what he meant.

In this way I learnt from Jonny something important about the relationship between the interior act of worship and the outward form. Outward form will seldom do justice to the substance of the interior prayer. A person's words will seldom exhaust the meaning of the prayer being prayed. This is often evidenced in various kinds of linguistic frustration which people exhibit in prayer.

## CONSTIPATED PRAYER

In my last church a motley assortment of twenty or so people used to come every Thursday to our lunchtime service. They were a good bunch and there was always great joy and earnestness evident in our times of prayer. There was also great variety in the language in which people expressed their prayers. Some, for instance, who were usually perfectly lucid and eloquent, would suddenly be reduced to a series of repetitions of 'O Lord we really just . . . just really . . . praise you. Oh praise you Lord!' and not much else in terms of words. Whereas others who again were perfectly normal and contemporary in their everyday speech would suddenly regress several hundred years, becoming sons and daughters of the seventeenth or even sixteenth century—all '-est' and '-eth' and endless dependent clauses! But both forms of prayer were infused with enthusiasm and sincerity. So why the language shift?

We could perhaps term the syndrome 'constipated prayer'! One person has a heartfelt prayer trying to get out, but, knowing that his normal register of speech will be woefully inadequate to express it, may opt for the richer, more resonant language of Cranmer or the Authorized

Version. Someone else, likewise, has a heartfelt prayer desperately trying to get out. 'Really', 'just' and 'O Lord' are expressions of linguistic frustration as the mind races round itself desperately trying to find words to express the prayer.

In the two cases, of course, neither will have been able to exhaust the whole meaning of the prayer by the words used. The words, whatever brand they are, will just have to serve here as a token or a symbol.

## TIMES AND TYPES

Spontaneous or extempore prayer comes into its own when—as in the cases above—the mind, imagination and emotions are moved or inspired, be it by joy or by anger, enthusiasm or despair. Then the mouth speaks what the heart thinks (Matthew 12.34)—the prayer of the heart being at the forefront of one's consciousness. For this reason spontaneous prayer is at its most useful when you actually have something to say.

There are times, however, especially during periods of dryness, when the heart seems to have nothing to say, and extempore prayer becomes rather lame—either just dribbling out rather pathetically or completely drying up. In times of spiritual buoyancy, the interior faculties are easily and spontaneously engaged by prayer. But in times of dryness and emptiness some help is needed in achieving this 'engagement'. This is the function of the 'prayer of attention'.

## TAKE A PRAYER

The idea of a prayer of attention is that you take a prayer and make it your own. You take the words and put yourself into them. The important thing is to choose a prayer that you agree with. Why? Because sometimes we pray out of feeling and sometimes out of conviction. In the desert experience, the feeling just isn't there. And that leaves us to pray out of our conviction. If you choose a prayer with which you agree on a profound level, then your praying of it will be sincere, even when the feeling and enthusiasm aren't there.

There are many prayers that you might use: prayers that saints have prayed through the centuries and treasured as being divinely inspired. You might think of the 'Our Father', the 'Grace', the 'Jesus Prayer', the Collect for Purity, or the Breastplate of St Patrick. There are many such prayers at our disposal—in compilations, in hymnbooks, in the Bible and in our prayer books. You could also write your own.

## BE SUCCINCT

Whatever you choose, it is best to take a short prayer, and one which, however you are feeling, you can pray with conviction. Brevity and succinctness in prayer is a virtue to which we are exhorted by many of the great teachers of the Church down the ages. For instance in *The Way of a Pilgrim* the anonymous pilgrim is given this advice:

> If you want (prayer) to be pure, right, and enjoyable, you must choose some sort of prayer consisting of few but forcible words and repeat it frequently for a long while. Then you will find delight in prayer.[2]

Our words of prayer, then, are to be few but forcible. And this indeed characterizes the treasured liturgical prayers of the Church. There is certainly succinctness, resonance and force to the words of the 'Our Father', the 'Jesus Prayer' or the Aaronic Blessing (Numbers 6.24–6). This is important, because in a prayer of attention each word or sense unit should provide a focus for attention—something we can think and imagine as we speak it. The

94

words should be few so as to focus our minds, rather than give us a hundred and one different things to think about. This is what St John Climacus means when he says 'An excessive multitude of words in prayer disperses the mind in dreams, while one word or a short sentence helps collect the mind' (*The Ladder of Divine Ascent*).

The object of such prayer is, as John Climacus puts it, to 'collect the mind'. This is part of what is meant by many of the Church Fathers when they speak of achieving a state of recollection. It is a place of greater consciousness, a place where prayer can begin to go deeper.

The prayer of attention is a good 'bridge' to a state of recollection, especially when we are feeling tired, weak, worried or confused. At such a time you might find it helpful, as well as using liturgical prayer, to write a prayer of your own—perhaps to cover something more specific. But make it extremely brief—in postcard or telegram form. Using such a form to express your prayer will help collect or focus the mind, and so bring you to a place of greater stillness.

## NOW PRAY

Having chosen a suitable prayer, the thing to do is pray it. That is to say we are to read it to God, putting ourselves into it and offering it to God. Metropolitan Anthony gives these words of guidance as to how to go about it:

> The Early Fathers and the whole of the Orthodox Tradition teach us that we must concentrate with an effort of will on the words of prayer we pronounce. We must pronounce the words attentively, matter of factly, without trying to create any sort of emotional state, and we must leave it to God to arouse whatever response we are capable of . . . Concentrate on the words so that you bring to God seriously, soberly, respectfully, words of prayer which you are conscious of and not an offering that is not yours because you were not aware of it.[3]

And so a prayer of attention is a prayer in which we are to become deeply aware, profoundly conscious of what it is we are praying. And that will be the result if we take note of the basic guidelines that Metropolitan Anthony makes above. Perhaps we could highlight three particular key words in making the prayer of attention work: Our praying and repetition of the prayer should be done (i) soberly; (ii) attentively; (iii) seriously.

(i) Soberly—This means without trying to create a feeling, an emotion or an atmosphere. That is to be left to God. Neither is the prayer a kind of dramatic reading. The words should be pronounced matter of factly.
(ii) Attentively—This means actually focusing our concentration on each word—imagining and thinking each word as we say it, becoming conscious of the meanings of each word.
(iii) Seriously—This means that this is in no way a casual or half-hearted exercise. It is one requiring a bit of effort. It is by an exercise of the will that we make the words our own and offer them to God.

The prayer should be repeated in this way for a chosen time. It is a general rule, after all, that if you want to do something well, do it often. The repetition of the prayer serves as a repeated 'conscientization' of the continuous and silent interior prayer of the heart. This is to say that the repetition brings the prayer to consciousness.


TRUE PRAYERS

The merit of using a personally composed prayer in this way lies in its specificity. The merit of liturgical prayers lies in their reliability. For if a prayer has become incorporated into the liturgy of the Church, this will probably have happened for a good reason. It may be syntactic structure which makes the prayer easily prayed. It may be poetic resonance that stimulates the mind, or a simple down-to-earthness that makes it eminently easy to relate to. Most importantly, the Church will have adopted the prayer, believing it to be a prayer truly inspired by the Holy Spirit.

In praying the words of the prayer, we are thus enabled to pray in truth and in accordance with the prayer of the Holy Spirit, even when our individual perception is weak. Through liturgical prayers we are united with the prayers of the Church as a whole and with the prayers of the Holy Spirit, even at the times when our awareness of those realities is somewhat limited. Praying in this way can do something to build that awareness.

As a way of prayer, the prayer of attention can be an enormous help to someone undergoing the desert experience. It is one of the most workable forms of prayer for the desert. It is a form which equips us in the art of recollection, moving us from emptiness and torpor to a place of stillness and undivided consciousness. This is the place where prayer can begin to go deeper.

# 15

## *PRAYING WITH THE HOLY SPIRIT*

*The Spirit helps us in our weakness.*

ROMANS 8.26

One of the most wonderful things about the mystery of prayer can be seen in this: that Jesus Christ, prayer and 'Jo(e) Christian' can all, at one level, be defined in the same way. For each can rightly be described as the place where humanity and divinity meet. It is true of Christ, of prayer and of any Christian.

At the heart of the gospel lies the truth that Jesus was and is the supreme meeting place of humanity and divinity—being himself both God and man. This is the meaning of the doctrine of the incarnation. And we have already been speaking of prayer being a meeting place or an encounter between the human and the divine. We have also been thinking of the Christian as such a meeting place. Jesus himself described the Christian as God's home (John 14), and St Paul speaks repeatedly of the Holy Spirit being 'put into our hearts'. What does Paul mean by this? Does he mean that the Spirit of God lives in a little portion of the Christian's body—i.e. the cardiovascular muscle? I think not. I think his words 'into our hearts' is a metaphor for the centre of our personhood, God within the very fabric of our being. Again Paul says, 'Don't you know that your body is the temple of the Holy Spirit?' Now, a temple is a special place where people go in order to be closer to the presence of God. And Paul is saying, 'You are that temple.' In other words you couldn't possibly get any closer to God. That is why the Church Fathers could say 'God is closer to you than your own breath.'

You are the temple of God. And wherever you are, God is. If that weren't incredible enough by itself, its full significance for prayer only becomes apparent when we remember that prayer is actually something that is going on within God himself. Prayer is something that God does!

You may be familiar with the picture that the New Testament gives us of the ascended Lord Jesus Christ being seated at the right hand of God the Father, praying for us and for all the saints. St Paul writes: 'Christ Jesus, who died—more than that, who was raised to life—is at the right hand of God, and is also interceding for us' (Romans 8.34). God the Son is praying—to God the Father—for us!

And likewise the Holy Spirit—as we see earlier in the passage:

> In the same way, the Spirit helps us in our weaknesses. We do not know what we ought to pray for, but the Spirit himself intercedes for us with groans that words cannot express. And he who searches our hearts knows the mind of the Spirit, because the Spirit intercedes for the saints in accordance with God's will. (Romans 8.26–7)

God the Holy Spirit is praying—to God the Father—for us!

I have to conclude, then, that when I pray it is not me who initiates the prayer. I am actually joining in with something that God is already doing. I can therefore never pray alone, because God himself is praying with me. What an extraordinary thing!

Since I am a temple of God's Spirit, and since the Spirit is one who prays, this means that wherever I am, prayer is! Wherever I am, God the Holy Spirit is praying for me without ceasing. Wherever I may be, and however I may feel, prayer is alive within me. That's the truth! Part of the Holy Spirit's job is to keep alive that ceaseless flow of prayer from ourselves to God, even when we are helpless to join in. Prayer from the heart is thus a constant reality—more constant than our own ability or will to pray.

Prayer is not something which we create. It is already there. It is a flame that God himself keeps burning within us. It burns at the very core, within the very fabric of our being. Our task is to lighten ourselves with its light and join in with its constant prayer.

What does all this imagery mean? It means that prayer is never something which we do alone. It is in that sense never a private or independent activity. It means, reassuringly, that even when our own prayer seems dead, prayer is, thanks to God, actually alive within us. It also means that we can move away from one idea of prayer—that I pray and consequently God makes himself present and joins with me—to the idea that God is praying and I am to make myself present to him and join with him! Indeed, making ourselves present to God is what the last few chapters have all been about.

The liberating thing to grasp is that, by grace, prayer is something in which we are caught up. Our task is to tune into that reality, to become aware of it, so that we can best join in. We might call this 'conscientization'.

## CONSCIENTIZATION

Everything that I have just said is enshrined for me in the symbol of the candle. It symbolizes the invisible reality, the prayer rising from me to God, even before I manage to still myself or open my mouth to pray.

Such an awareness goes some way towards putting our words of prayer into proper perspective. We use our words of prayer to make our prayer conscious, aimed and specific. The words themselves are just the tip of the iceberg, a meagre manifestation of a much deeper reality. This perspective helps us to make sense of using short prayers, often repeated, such as the Lord's Prayer, or the ancient prayer:

Holy God, holy and strong,
Holy and immortal, have mercy upon us.

Their repetition, according to the Eastern Orthodox practice is not a 'vain repetition' of the same prayer—because the prayer does not equal the words. Rather the repetition of the words is a repeated 'conscientization' of the silent prayer continually rising up from the heart. It is on this understanding that I sometimes use set or liturgical prayers in my intercessions.

The 'Jesus Prayer' for example is highly suitable for such a manner of intercession:

Lord Jesus Christ, Son of God,
Have mercy upon my sister/brother *N*.

The words focus the prayer both on the Lord Jesus Christ, the Son of God, and upon whoever *N* is. The phrase that joins them is the plea 'have mercy'. The strength of this prayer lies both in its brevity and in its breadth: that phrase 'have mercy' can embrace so many different desires and hopes and prayers that we may want to bring before God for that person. Its strength is that it can mean so much.

However, having repeated it a few times, I may be aware that there is in fact something more specific that I want to pray for the person, which 'have mercy' doesn't quite convey. And so I might just add a brief phrase such as:

Lord Jesus Christ, Son of God,
Have mercy upon my brother Stuart,
Give him strength and faith . . .

or,

Lord Jesus Christ, Son of God,
Have mercy upon my sister Esther
And heal her . . .

Limiting the initial wording to that of the basic prayer, again helps you become more conscious of what your urgent prayer is for the person, and so you pray it with much more of yourself behind the few forceful words. It thus becomes a more thoroughly focused prayer.

This is another traditional prayer which can be used as a set form in intercession:

> Most merciful God, thy will be done which would have all men to be saved and to come unto knowledge of the truth; save and help your servant *N*. Take this desire of mine as a token of the love which thou hast ordained, and in thy tender mercy, hear my prayer.

The very wording of this prayer reminds me that it is this silent desire of my heart, rather than the spoken words, that make it a real prayer. I am using the words, therefore, simply as a vocalization of the silent prayer of my heart for whoever *N* is. I may experience that silent prayer as a feeling, or as an image, or a longing, or even as tears. Or I may not. The words are there merely as a verbal frame to help me be conscious of my prayer for *N* and so make it a much deeper and more integrated prayer.

Spoken prayer, whether extempore or set and repeated is, for us, a conscientization of the silent and invisible reality, that of the prayer of the Spirit within our hearts, which is there and alive even when our feelings are telling us the contrary. When we speak, or move, or feel in prayer we are joining with the Spirit who is our prayer partner and our invisible strength. Thus we pray with him. And thus he helps us in our weakness.

# 16

## PRAYING WITH HEAVEN

*Elisha prayed, 'O Lord open his eyes that he may see!'*

2 KINGS 6.17

We have just seen in the previous chapter, that when we pray we are not alone; we are joining with God. But more than that, as we declare in the Eucharistic prayer, in our prayer and worship we are joining 'with angels and arch-angels, and with all the company of heaven'. Indeed we are surrounded, in the words of the writer to the Hebrews, by 'a great cloud of witnesses'.

The Book of Revelation paints for us a picture of the constant flow of worship which rises to God from the saints of the Most High, from angels, archangels, cheru-bim and seraphim. It is an ongoing reality, independent of us, but one in which we can join ourselves by entering into prayer. In that sense prayer is always corporate. This perspective is reflected in the words of H.F. Lyte's mar-vellous hymn, 'Praise my soul the King of heaven'. It con-cludes with these words:

> Angels, help us to adore him;
> Ye behold him face to face;
> Sun and moon, bow down before him,
> Dwellers all in time and space:
> Praise him! Praise him!
> Praise him! Praise him!
> Praise, with us, the God of grace.

The words of this hymn set our worship within the con-text of a great crowd of witnesses. Some liturgies—such as those of the Eastern Church—are strong in emphasizing our partnership with heaven in prayer and worship. And in

103

liturgical prayers such as the following one, we both acknowledge and invite that partnership:

> O Lord, our Master and our God, You have appointed the heavenly orders and the hosts of angels and archangels to minister to your glory.
> Grant that your holy angels may accompany us, minister with us and glorify your goodness.[1]

Similarly the canticle we call the *Benedicite* catalogues a whole host of agents responsible with us for the worship of God—as indeed do many of the psalms. In the *Benedicite* (or 'A Song of Creation') we acknowledge and invite worship from people and powers—even creation itself:

> O ye Angels of the Lord . . .
> O ye Heavens . . .
> O all ye Powers of the Lord . . .
> O ye Sun and Moon . . .
> O all ye Green Things upon the earth . . .
> O all ye Beasts and Cattle . . .
> O ye Priests of the Lord . . .
> O ye Servants of the Lord . . .
> O ye Spirits and Souls of the Righteous . . .

Whether in a worshipping congregation or alone in our room, when we pray we make ourselves part of this vast, time-transcending wave of worship rebounding to God from the creation he has made. Again the liturgy of the Eucharist sums it up well; when addressing God we celebrate our communion or oneness 'with all who stand before you in earth and heaven, we worship you, Father almighty, in songs of everlasting praise.'

We acknowledge and celebrate the fact of our joining with heaven in worship, when we use the songs and acclamations from the Book of Revelation or from Isaiah, for example, in hymns, choruses or liturgy—such as in the acclamation that follows those words we have just quoted:

> Blessing and honour and glory and power
> be yours for ever and ever. Amen.

These songs are being sung already. When we sing them, we are simply joining in!

The vision described in the Book of Revelation tells us yet more about the corporate nature of prayer and worship.

In Revelation 5 and 8, we are given a picture of fragrant incense rising to God. This, says the writer, symbolizes the prayers of the saints—which, in his terminology, refers to all Christians, i.e. the whole Church spanning time and space. From the heavenly perspective, our own individual or congregational prayers make us a part of that timeless billow in heaven, part of that cloud of worship which has been rising up to God from across the world for thousands upon thousands of years. This is the reality of which we are just a part.

St Paul also writes of this time-transcending oneness of the Church, when he symbolizes the Church Universal as the very body of Christ. In the ASB liturgy we rejoice in this truth every time we celebrate the Eucharist:

*President*: We break this bread
To share in the body of Christ.

*All*: Though we are many, we are one body,
because we all share in one bread.

This essential unity of Christ's body is not one divided or segregated by time. That is to say the acclamation is not just true of those who happen to be present, or alive at the time that it is said. It is true of all who are in Christ. We are one body because we all share in one bread. The body of Christ transcends the apparent barriers of time and space. And so I can know that I am one in Christ's body with St Paul, with St John the Evangelist, St John of the Cross, St Seraphim of Sarov, with Isaac Watts, Martin Luther, and indeed all my sisters and brothers in the faith across the sweep of time.

This oneness with the Church Universal and

throughout time, is part of the meaning of the icons to be found on the ceilings, stands and iconostases of Eastern Orthodox churches. These are not merely portraits of long-dead heroes or absent friends. Quite the reverse, in fact! They are there to remind us that we, in our worship, are joining with these people, one in Christ with them. It is oneness or communion, rather than our separation, that such icons are intended to convey.

This is also part of the symbolism of incense in Christian prayer. It is there to remind us that our prayer and worship is somehow an organic part of the worship of the whole Church across time and space. We worship in each other's midst.

The Franciscan prayer book sets our worship in this same context by including this prayer before the saying of the office:

> We adore you, most Holy Lord Jesus Christ,
> Here, and in all your churches throughout the world.
> And we bless you, because by your holy cross
> You have redeemed the world.

Set prayers, incense and icons can help build our awareness of our part within the whole body of Christ. But so can the use for prayer of the liturgy of the Church—the divine offices, prayer books etc. By praying, for instance, the order for Morning Prayer, or for Compline, the individual believer is uniting him or herself with hundreds of thousands across the world and across time, who, from a divine perspective, are praying with us. By praying prayers that the Church has collected, prayed and translated down the centuries, we are, in a very real way, joining in with hundreds of thousands of saints, both contemporary and departed, brothers and sisters who are our fellows and partners in Christ. This is what the 'communion of saints' should mean for us.

Being aware of this transcendent, corporate dynamic to prayer can be an incredibly helpful and freeing thing.

Realizing I am one of many takes off a lot of pressure. Indeed many people go through the life of prayer with a lot of unnecessary pressure, treating it like some terrible lonesome journey. It is not. Prayer, in every way, puts us in good company. We need to wake up to this—especially in the West where so much is made of individual effort. The truth is, being a Christian makes us one of a team, both a visible and an invisible one. So let us echo the words of the prophet Elisha, 'O Lord open our eyes that we may see.'

# 17

# *STIMULATING PRAYER*

*We must develop our skill as carefully as an artist if we want to live intimately with Jesus.*

THOMAS À KEMPIS[1]

In the previous chapters we have already seen how different senses may be made part of our experiencing of prayer; we have thought particularly of how vision, smell, hearing and feeling might be involved in the doing of prayer. Engaging our senses in prayer is a direct way of including more of ourselves—more of what makes us human people—in the doing of prayer. Indeed all the sensory faculties can be used in prayer. A Communion service can engage all five. Six if you include a sense for the 'other' or the supernatural! The use of visual and musical art will engage the eyes and ears, the use of incense will involve the sense of smell. I may represent prayers by my body in kneeling, or genuflecting, raising hands, making a sign of the cross, walking to the communion rail, or even in prostration. The bread and wine are things I can see and taste. Words and ideas may involve my intellect. The symbolic may speak to me at a level of consciousness beyond words, and with my intuition I may sense God's special presence.

If I want a person to person encounter with God, then all that makes me a person should be involved in the act of prayer. Churches that emphasize art and beauty in the place and practice of worship provide ways of involving the whole of the worshipper in this kind of way.

Some churches shy away from this attitude and use both buildings and forms of worship that are as dour as possible—deliberately plain and unstimulating. You don't have to travel far before you come across a church building

108

which seems to have been designed with the express purpose of saying 'He is not here!' or 'This is not a special place!' This is especially sad to see in drab and grey postwar urban settings, where all the buildings seem to be saying the same thing: 'This is not a special place!' The environment for prayer will seldom be neutral. It will either foster prayerfulness or it will not.

Historically it has been the 'high' churches which have placed an emphasis on art and beauty in the place and practice of worship. And we should note that it was principally in the barrenness of the inner city areas of the nineteenth century that these churches thrived. In part the employment of art was made to convey a certain theology of worship. The belief that in worship we are united in the communion of the saints and with the hosts of angels and archangels is one that has been central to Catholic and Eastern Orthodox traditions. And sacred art and architecture in those traditions—particularly in the East—have sought to communicate symbolically this idea of the joining together of heaven and earth—hence the use of icons from very early times, the use of incense and Byzantine-style decorations on walls and ceilings.

Time and again history has seen great iconoclastic movements which have sought to strip away a use of art (and ultimately of money) which they have seen as over-indulgent, vulgar, or idolatrous. One cannot deny that to some degree such iconoclasm might have been warranted at certain times and in certain places. But this legacy has left many modern Western Christians, especially those in Protestant Churches, with a deep and sometimes irrational suspicion of any kind of art, symbol or ritual—whether in public worship or private prayer.

In many churches no appeal is made to any part of the person in the pew other than to his or her intellectual faculties. The forms of worship, the style of prayer, the conventions of dress and the building itself are often deliberately made as plain and unstimulating as possible. There is a strong element of this even today in mainstream Protestant religion in this country.

This kind of spirituality is often brought in the Christian's mind into the private practice of prayer. And so no attention will be paid to the environment chosen for prayer, and no faculty other than the intellect will be involved. The reason this is so unhealthy is that it denies and excludes from the prayer situation most of our faculties, most of the things which make us conscious!

It is not just with our minds that we are to pray. There is enough in the Bible to tell us this:

> I will pray with my spirit, but I will also pray with my mind. (1 Corinthians 14.15)

> Offer your bodies as living sacrifices, holy and pleasing to God—this is your spiritual act of worship. (Romans 12.1b)

> Love the LORD your God with all your heart and with all your soul and with all your strength. (Deuteronomy 6.5)

If your usual form of prayer seems empty, then invest some thought in how you might make it an exercise that stimulates and engages more of your personality. It may be that your current custom of prayer is denying or excluding whole aspects of your humanity. And so the emptiness you are experiencing may again not be God's absence but your own partial absence!


MAKE A MEAL OF IT

When prayer is empty, as it is at the onset of the desert experience, we have seen that in many different ways our need is to engage more of ourselves in the doing of it—that is to say to try and pray as an integrated, whole person. And in previous chapters we have already explored this necessary integration of what we might term our hearts, souls, minds and bodies. In this chapter we have been thinking of engaging the senses and the aesthetic in prayer. Some people might be concerned at this point that such a use of aesthetic or symbolic environment might detract or distract from direct encounter with God. But this need not be the case. Indeed we could liken detail of this sort in prayer to the preparation of a meal.

If a host is preparing a pleasant evening meal for a guest and wants to make it special, then he will do more than simply prepare food. He will of course want the food to be of fine quality, crafted by his own hand (though maybe pre-prepared in parts!). But furthermore he will want the room to look clean, relatively tidy and be of a suitable temperature. He will ensure that the table is comfortably and suitably arranged; that the lighting is pleasant and (probably) subdued; that the place looks, feels and smells nice. He may add some soft music to enhance the ambience.

Now especially if this is an intimate supper for two that the host is preparing, in no sense will he have made these secondary arrangements to distract from the all-important guest. Quite the reverse, in fact. He has simply created an environment that is fitting to the occasion. We should perhaps make similar efforts when it comes to our appointments for prayer. The environment can be used to foster a sense of prayerfulness—just as it can foster a mellow, romantic mood. And, as in the case of the meal, such efforts are not a distraction from our invisible divine guest. Quite the reverse. Our efforts will have an effect upon ourselves and help us to show God that meeting with him in prayer is a special appointment for us.

That is why in my room I have made a special place where I pray. It is not that I can't or may not pray elsewhere—indeed I do! It's just that in this alcove I have made the effort to create an environment that helps me to be still and remember God, to be comfortable and prayer-ful. Indeed, by going and kneeling there I am making a physical prayer—a concrete statement that says 'Here I am

111

Lord. I am coming before you. I am wanting to pray.' This personal place of sounds, smells, images and sensations—as well as those of nature all around—serves not as a distraction from prayer, but a stimulus to it.

In times of dryness, it would be a mistake to keep prayer as plain and unstimulating a practice as possible. In the desert I need all the help I can get! We should instead stop and consider whether there is anything we might do to make prayer a less dull activity for us. We should put the same kind of creative thought into our devotions that we would into preparing an intimate meal. This is after all the imagery of Revelation 3.20: Christ offers himself to anyone who hears and receives him. And the image of the fellowship he offers is that of a meal. So let us put this imagery to work when we invite Christ into our midst by the act of prayer. We shall explore in the following chapter practical ways in which we might do this.

# 18

# *USING SYMBOLS*

The Church can be a very wordy place to live. Christians can be very wordy people. There are perhaps two reasons why we in the West often fall into an unhealthy over-obsession with words. First because we have been concerned with guarding the truths of the faith. And since doctrine has generally been defined through polemic, and sometimes bitter and violent polemic, the process of formulation itself has often multiplied and lengthened words—words intended to define doctrine in order to exclude heresy. Secondly because in the West great emphasis has been placed upon verbal intellect as being the autonomous 'real' self. And words are the workhorse of the verbal intellect. Words have been treated as the only 'objective' or 'safe' medium. They have been venerated as if they were an absolute medium—which they are not.

However the advent of the desert experience to an individual often dislodges words from their central role (as we saw in the chapter on detachment). In the desert, words seem to be of less use, and so silence comes. Indeed it is often through the desert journey that the disciple learns the art and discipline of silence. And it is often out of the exercise of silence that we come to a deeper understanding of other forms of prayer: forms utilizing the power of silence and of symbols.

Experience of dryness and emptiness in my own practice of prayer has brought me personally to a greater appreciation of symbolic forms of prayer: physical prayer (expression through physical posture or movement), candles, icons, incense, photographs and pictures have all taken a part in strengthening my life of prayer and helping it to survive the desert journey.

The symbolic plays a profound role, not only in bolstering the practice of prayer, but in taking it onto a different level. As we have already seen, our words only reflect a tiny proportion of reality and a tiny proportion of prayer. The symbolic plays a vital role in bringing about a deeper conscientization of the reality of prayer. We shall see how this relates to various forms—specifically, the use of environment, candles, photographs, icons, incense and pictures.

ENVIRONMENT

Natural beauty can elicit a response from most people. Even the least poetic of us can be inspired by the sight of a mountainscape, a landscape or a seascape. The greatness of creation stands as testimony to the Creator, a symbol of his glory. The psalmist writes:

> The heavens declare the glory of God; the skies proclaim the work of his hands. Day after day they pour forth speech; night after night they display knowledge. There is no speech or language where their voice is not heard. Their voice goes out into all the earth, their words to the end of the world. (Psalm 19.1–4)

Perhaps the psalmist had been inspired by a brilliant sunrise or a fantastic night sky when he wrote this psalm. Here is a very personal response to visiting a place which I find very beautiful. It is near the village of Drewsteignton in mid-Devon:

> As I stand
> There's a power coursing through my veins;
> Strange Empathy;
> A sensation I can not explain.
> This incredible space makes me feel so small.
> Yet within, and with
> Brother Son.

Standing tall
On a hill—a windy hilltop high;
Vast Sky—often sun and moon and stars above.
And the majesty of nature down below
Makes me feel, makes me feel
Brother Son.

Stand in awe!
The power of history is here.
I await the author of all the years,
Whose eternity makes me feel so small,
Yet beheld, and held.
Brother Son!

Let me shout!
Let me bellow out, loud and free,
And reach out to touch this sweet mystery!
Sweet simplicity, the kindness of your arms
Makes me feel, makes me feel
This Strange Empathy;
And the kindness of your arms
Makes me feel, makes me feel
Brother Son.


This poem speaks of my experience of an inspirational
place. It's a high hill looking down across Devon through
the folds of the countryside. It's the kind of place which
quite of itself generates a sense of God's power and closeness. And in such places, not only God, but also our own
prayer, can feel close and natural. In places of great space
and beauty, prayer often comes quite naturally. Woods,
high hills, seascapes, mountainscapes, landscapes, sunrises
and sunsets; these places and sights quite gently but po-
tently put us in touch with prayer, not through appealing
to the verbal intellect, but by touching us at a much deeper
level of consciousness.

Natural beauty, then, is something that we can use to
help us pray when our prayerfulness is on a low. If you live
in the countryside, then you have an advantage not to be
wasted. If there are places you can easily get to, where you

find yourself more prayerful, then make the most of them. For instance, every twelve months I try to make a retreat for prayer and quiet to a place in Crawley Down in Sussex. One of the reasons that I find this such a good place is that in addition to the wonderful relaxing atmosphere of quiet and prayer at the monastery itself, it is completely surrounded by the most lovely woodland. The natural quiet but alive atmosphere of those woods has helped me to pray at times when I have otherwise felt far from God and unable to pray. The beauty of those woods helps me to be aware of God and of the prayer of my heart.

Rather nearer to home, there is a golf course just a stone's throw away. It's nothing beautiful like that hill in Devon, or the woodland in Sussex, but it's a local bit of green space that I rather appreciate. The enjoyment of that environment makes the walk across the golf course a naturally easy place to pray—even with the distraction of having to pay close attention to where I'm treading! I make the return walk about once a day and use it rather like a mini-retreat.

A good church building is a place of quiet and restful beauty. Some, sadly, are not. But in the noise and dirt of the inner city an open church can be a sanctuary for peace and an atmosphere of prayerfulness. And the sense of the sacred, that the smells and sounds and art of such places provide, makes them good places to go and collect yourself to pray. Again this can be a mini-retreat.

But as well as in nature and in church buildings, the symbolic is very much at home—at home! Candles, photographs, icons, incense and pictures: these can all be of help in private prayer. All are symbols, pointing beyond themselves to a more profound reality. They communicate in ways unique to symbols, which words cannot equal. Through the symbolic we relate to reality in ways not possible via other means. They engage not just the mind, but a yet deeper level of consciousness.

## CANDLES

Candles have a quiet beauty all their own. They are able to help us to become still and collected. Contemplating the silent dance of the burning flame has a gentle therapeutic effect, and calms us down while holding the attention rather than lulling us to sleep. Furthermore, focusing one's gaze upon a candle burning in a darkened room diminishes the field of vision and so helps close our eyes to distractions. In these ways, then, we can use candles as a way of focusing our attention and achieving a state of recollection.

But they also point to something beyond themselves. The Church generally uses candles in two ways. On or over an altar, the candle reminds us of the eternal presence of God with us. As votive candles, they represent for us our own ongoing silent prayer, and the prayers of other saints.

My own use of candles in private prayer embraces both these ideas. The candle serves to remind me of the constant and unceasing prayer that God has set within me by the gift of the Holy Spirit. It reminds me, as I quieten myself, that the praying of the Holy Spirit is there already as something of which I can become conscious and with which I can resonate and join my prayers.

Thus, with the help of the candle's quiet light, I become 'recollected'. And with the help of the candle as a symbol, I become more conscious of the Spirit who is my prayer partner.


## PHOTOGRAPHS

It is chiefly in keeping intercession going that I have found photographs of especial help. About half the people I pray for on a regular basis are on the walls of my room—that is to say, their photographs are. I put it that way, because

117

that is how people talk about photographs. We relate to photographs all the time as the symbols that they are. Somebody opens his wallet and shows you a photograph, saying, '*This* is my little daughter'. And he'll sit looking at the photograph and remember how fond he is of his little girl. That's how photos work. And that's how they can work in prayer. Photographs are far more evocative of the memory or feeling of a person than a dry list of names. And so as I move from picture to picture, I have the person I'm praying for much more fully in heart and mind than if I'd just read the name off a list.

Not only am I made more fully conscious of the person being prayed for, but, like the man with the picture in his wallet, I am also made more aware of what my desire or prayer is for that person. Thus I become more conscious of my own intercession for that person, and my prayer becomes a much richer, more profound exercise. Having become more aware of the essence of my prayer, I may then express it—which might be in extempore or liturgical form. The advantage of a short repeated liturgical form of words is that it eliminates the waffle-factor and will not detract from the state of recollection. A short repeated prayer better maintains the consciousness of the prayer which the photograph has helped evoke and focus.

ICONS AND INCENSE

Icons or sacred art can work in a similar way to photographs. Like a photograph an icon is a symbol of the person depicted. But in a traditional icon, the symbolism will be much richer.

The little Russian icon of Christ that I keep in my prayer corner serves—like a photograph in a wallet—to remind me of the reality of Christ and of my relationship with him.

It reminds me that, as I pray, I am actually speaking to another human being—Jesus. And like the photographs in my intercessions, having a picture of Christ helps put me in touch with my desire and feelings for Christ and my prayer to him. When I have no words to offer, then I have a symbol of Christ to contemplate as the silent prayer of the Spirit within me continues, unceasing. My kneeling in contemplation makes physical expression of my silent prayer of self-offering to him.

Of course Christ is not the only person to figure in sacred art or iconography. Indeed in my room I have portraits and icons of some of the saints. They are not only there as tributes to, and reminders of, people I honour and respect for their lives and example; they are not only there as reminders of absent friends. They are there to remind me that when I take my stand before God in prayer and worship to him, I join with these people, one in Christ with them, the unity of Christ's body breaking every barrier. It is the mysterious closeness of these sisters and brothers from across time and not their absence that these pictures and icons signify.

Incense, too, evokes this sense of the communality of prayer. It reminds me that in my praying I take my stand before God as an organic part of his whole Church spanning time and space. This cosmic flow of prayer and worship is symbolized in the Revelation of St John in the image of incense, sweet and fragrant, rising before God in the heavens (Revelation 5.8; 8.4).

The Church has adopted the same image to depict the reality of joining 'with angels and archangels and with all the company of heaven'. The incense makes the statement via the eyes, and nose. Standing in a faint cloud of fragrant incense symbolizes our communion with all the saints and with heaven itself. The symbol represents the unseen mystery that, in Christ, we are somehow in each other's midst.

119

PICTURES

The symbol of the candle embraces all the thought and consciousness of our chapter on praying with the Holy Spirit. The symbol of an icon can embrace a whole body of thought and feeling concerning our relationship with Christ and with his Church. The symbol of incense embraces all the thought and consciousness of our chapter on praying with heaven.

In the same way, a picture can embrace, convey, evoke a whole body of truth, thought and feeling. Again through the power of symbolism, pictures can engage our personality at a level deeper than that of words. And just as meditating on sacred words can be a bridge of understanding between us and a revealed truth, meditating on sacred art can provide us a similar bridge—but, again, on a different level. In a sense, the truth which a picture might convey is not merely within in the picture. It is within you. The picture resonates with what is in you and re-evokes your feeling or consciousness of that truth. The picture is then a means of 'conscientization'—to use my buzz word.

The act of contemplating a picture of this kind is like a mental chewing of the cud—chewing it over for purposes of further nutrition. The cud (which stands for the body of truth which we already have) is already within. Chewing (which stands for contemplation) is the means of nourishing ourselves further by it.

If I were to sit down and explain everything I believe about silence in prayer, the location of prayer, the concept of peace, the value of stillness, the way of recollection, the concept of 'retreat' and encounter with God, it would take a long time and an awful lot of words. But all those thoughts, and doctrines, together with the associations and feelings, are stimulated and appealed to by one of the pictures in my prayer corner. It is a picture of a cloister. Just to look for any length of time at this picture begins to make me aware and conscious of that whole body of thought and feeling. Inded, just seeing the picture in my mind's eye can do the same. That is to describe just one of the pictures I use. There are others I could describe: the picture of a church, a monastery, a long dirt road, a man in a desert, a picture of a flower, an abstract representation of a candle, a sleeping child embraced in a hand. They are all symbolic in various ways, and can appeal to the heart in a very direct way. That is the value of symbols; they not only communicate very effectively, but they can represent the unrepresentable, point us to the transcendent and make us more profoundly conscious of the invisible. They are tools in the way of conscientization.

# 19

# *GOD-CONSCIOUSNESS*

*Knowing God is . . . a shift of consciousness, a reversal of the natural mode of thinking, or, better yet, a conversion of attention.*

RICHARD WOODS[1]

The desert experience is supremely an experience of change. As we have seen, it will involve a change in experience, a change in expectation, a change in understanding, and change in prayer. Indeed our whole being is affected. The essential change which the desert should effect is a new and greater consciousness of God.

Our first perception of the desert or the dark night is that we are being starved of the 'sweet spiritual water' that we had been tasting. In other words all the ways in which we had become accustomed to experiencing God simply cease.

It is an interesting exercise to ask people how they most usually experience God, and where. You are likely to encounter a range of answers. People may say that it is in corporate worship, in a church building, in absolution, in a garden, in the bath, or in prayer meetings that they generally sense God as being most present. People may say they sense God's nearness by a feeling in their heart, in their heads, or hands, or face. Or they may speak of sensing a presence or a stillness. These are all perfectly valid ways in which different people at different times say they experience the special touch of God.

However if we put too much store by this level of experience we can make ourselves vulnerable to a particular trap. And that is to think and behave as if our experience of God were God himself, and come to look for God's presence only in our accustomed ways and places, as if God would only reveal himself to us in those ways and places. Thus God brings a certain kind of experience to us, and we try to box him within it.

While most Christians would want to affirm the ubiquity or omnipresence of God, many seem to live from spiritual 'fix' to 'fix'. This lifestyle may satisfy for a while, but what happens when the fixes run out? What happens when God stops revealing himself to you in the same way? This is what will happen at the onset of the desert or the dark night. At this point, believers may wake up to the reality that God is bigger than those experiences and is to be found outside them too. Or they will do their darnedest to work up or recreate their accustomed pattern of religious experience. They may give up altogether when they find this no longer possible. And that is an unnecessary tragedy.

The aim of the desert is not to torture the believer and see how long he or she can continue without another helping of religious experience! The aim is to bring the pilgrim to a much broader and more stable 'God-consciousness' which is far less tied to particular kinds of experience, and thus far less vulnerable to the inevitable changes in our patterns of experience. As we have already seen, our patterns of experience are affected by our general state of being. And that is dependent upon a hundred and one different factors.

The prerequisite to acquiring this greater God-consciousness is to let God out of the neat little box into which we often put him. And we have already thought a little about this in Chapter Seven (on Integration). The key is to acknowledge our ignorance of God, and to expect to find him in any and every situation. Indeed we must learn to expect the unexpected. Liberating ourselves of set expectation will allow us to see beyond our expectations.

What is true of our human relationships is often true of the way in which we relate to God. It is often the case that we do not relate directly to a person. Rather we relate to our *image* or *expectation* of that person. Now, most of the time we are not aware of the distinction, and we think we know the person. But from time to time the person will do something unexpected. And we say that they are acting out of character. But occasionally such behaviour will waken us up to the fact that we didn't know the person as well as we had thought. Our perception or image of the person hadn't been quite accurate. This is a normal and essential aspect in the process of getting to know somebody.

So long as we are aware of the limitedness of our knowledge of a person, then we will have a healthy relationship with them—be able to see them as they are. But as soon as we believe that we have somebody 'sussed' or boxed—'Oh, I know just what he's like!' or 'I know just how he thinks'—then we have stopped relating directly to the person, preferring to relate to our image of him or her, which can only ever be a caricature. If we let this happen, then we are effectively blinding ourselves to beholding new facets or new depths in the person concerned, and something in that relationship dies.

For instance we can probably all think of parents who never let their children grow up. Regardless of the actual age and maturity of their offspring, they go on relating to them as eternal twelve-year-olds. The television series *Sorry* depicts just such a situation. Timothy Lumsden can say, 'Mother, I'm forty-five' as often as he likes, but his mother will go on treating him like a naughty twelve-year-old, convinced that she knows 'just what he's like'.

In this situation it is obvious that Mrs Lumsden is not actually able to see Timothy as he is in reality. She will relate only to her inaccurate image of her son. It is her attachment to this image of her son that is, in fact, preventing her from seeing the reality: a sorry, frustrated forty-five-year-old. She persists in relating to her caricature of him because for her it is more comfortable to do so. She is too frightened to open her eyes and see the real son. Because the real son might not need her and might leave home. And this above all else is what she dreads and will not countenance.

This is not dissimilar to what can happen in our relationship with God. We think that we already know what he is like, and how he behaves. We have an image of him. If we become arrogantly confident in the accuracy of that image, it will actually prevent us from seeing God as he really is. Our set of expectations of him can blind us to seeing his greater reality. Perhaps we too are afraid to open our eyes. Frightened perhaps of letting go of the God we can predict, the God we have sussed, our familiar and tame God. But God is like C.S. Lewis's Aslan in the Narnia Chronicles—Aslan is a wild lion who cannot be tamed!

The desert or dark night may alert us to the fact that we may have tried to do this to God. It may be that our perception of God was accurate to our experience years ago, but no longer tallies with our present experience or understanding. Unless we can accept that we don't know God so well, and that this perception needs to be discarded or modified, then there is no hope that our knowledge of God will progress. We will have blinded ourselves to seeing new facets and new depths in God. And so something in that relationship dies.

When Moses asked God for his name, the Lord answered: 'I AM WHAT I AM' or, as some believe to be a better translation of the Hebrew: 'I WILL BE WHAT I WILL BE' (Exodus 3.14). The Jews attached enormous significance to names. The name and nature of a place or a person were very closely identified in Jewish thought. The Lord's reply to Moses is therefore a most enigmatic and tantalizing one. It is a stout refusal to be encompassed, defined, boxed or typecast. He is too great for that, too much of an enigma. God is *paradoxa*—which means beyond confinement, definition or imagining. This elusive name given by God to Moses should be of profound signficance to the way in which we think of God.

We need always to beware of having God typecast, of believing that we already know how God will reveal himself today. To believe that is to pray to a god whose name would be more like 'I WILL BE exactly how I seemed to you yesterday and the day before'! God is free to reveal himself however, wherever and whenever he should choose. If I cling tenaciously to my expectations, then I may very well miss him when he comes. If I think of God only as my celestial mate, then I will miss him when he comes to me as righteous Lord. If I think of him only as judge, then I will miss him when he comes to me as brother. If I think of him only as a father, then I will miss him when he comes to me as a mother. If I believe God only ever comes in overt and obvious ways, then I will miss him when he comes covertly and meekly. No matter how broad my picture of God, he will always be bigger. But the narrower my expectations are, the more I shall miss him when he comes to me.

AN ILLUSTRATION

I am told that the Queen is a wonderfully ordinary person when you meet her, and that she expertly puts people at relative ease. However it is inevitable that the Queen's encounter with her subjects will lack a certain naturalness or unaffectedness simply because she is the Queen. People's perception of her as royal, or even simply as being important, will unavoidably inhibit them. They will behave, and probably speak, quite differently from normal.

However I understand that the Queen has on occasions donned plain coat and scarf and has moved about incognito. Unless they were in the know or particularly wily, those with whom she mixed would fail to recognize her. After all people know what the Queen looks and dresses like, and that she does not move about freely. Because of their certainty on this, she would be quite invisible to them—although all the time she would be able to see them as they are in a way which would be impossible were she not so concealed.

Similarly Christ 'was in the world . . . and the world did not recognize him' (John 1). Indeed in the story of the separation of the sheep and the goats—as recorded in the Gospel of Matthew—the cry of both the righteous and unrighteous will be, 'Lord when did we see you . . .?' His reply comes: 'Whatever you did for one of the least of these brothers of mine, you did for me . . . Whatever you did not do for one of the least of these, you did not do for me.' Thus God has moved about us incognito. Thus he has tested, seen and known us. To us his presence may be anything beween concrete—'that which . . . we have seen with our eyes, which we have looked at and our hands have touched . . .' (1 John 1)—and invisible (as in Matthew 25). But his encounter with us has still been real. He has met with us—as we are!


AWARENESS

God is free to surprise us. To come to us in ever new and changing ways. The goal of the desert experience is the attainment of *diakrisis*. To attain *diakrisis* means to learn to recognize God when he comes—in whatever manner he may have chosen. Archimandrite Sophrony writes that God withdraws . . .

. . . in order that we might know the things that are freely given us from on high . . . Often, usually even, he varies the character of his coming, and thus I am continually enriched in the realm of the Spirit.[2]

*Diakrisis* is the discernment which enables us to recognize the movements of God and to become aware of 'things that are freely given us from on high', whatever they may be. It is, then, an awareness in the realm of the spirit—what Ephesians refers to as an 'enlightening of the eyes of our heart' (Ephesians 1.18).

We shall not see God as he is until we meet him in Glory—at the moment of our death, or at the final apocalypse. Then we shall see him face to face. In the meantime God works within us through the deserts and dark nights to bring us to greater consciousness and truer vision of him.

## BECOMING AWARE

The novices asked the Master for a word of wisdom.
'To grow in union with God,' he said, 'you must simply become aware.'
'What, Master, are we to be aware of?' they asked.
'But if I answered you this,' replied the Master, 'you would not be aware; you would be watching.'
'How is this any different?' they asked.
'Unless the heart is free from desire and expectation, watching will stop you seeing what there is, and so awareness dies.'

This story bears some truth. It is a natural reflex to filter our from our consciousness what we do not expect to see. For example it is much less likely that you would recognize your postman if you walked past him sunbathing on a beach in Uruguay, than if you walked past him delivering mail on your street. Expectation inevitably shapes what we see. True awareness happens when we can liberate what we see from what we expect to see. This mental discipline finds a home in practices common to various Eastern traditions.

The Celts, too, had a way of liberating their consciousness of God from narrow confines or expectations. And that was to associate God and God's immanence with everything seen and everything done, with every time, place and action. The hub of this spirituality or 'awakeness' lay in the practice of using prayers to accompany every commonplace occasion and activity. The prayers both declare and invite God's presence with them. The prayers were both earthy and poetic which lent them a sense of power, and made them easily memorable. The faith of the Celts was thus enormously practical, down to earth and supremely conscious of God. Avery Brooke writes:

> The Celts' sense of God's presence and power was so great because they saw God in everything, worshipped him through everything, and turned to him for aid and guidance in everything they did . . . We tend today . . . to think that the Celts 'just had' this faith. 'Weren't they lucky,' we say, 'that they had it to sustain them in their trials?' But I have come to believe that it was not luck. It was practice . . . We need to *practise* the presence of God.[3]

OCCASIONAL PRAYERS

We are wrong to assume that Celtic prayer can belong only to a lifestyle that is slow and simple—i.e. an imagined sixth-century lifestyle. This is not the case. Celtic prayers have enormous potential for Christians living in the modern world. Indeed prayers continue to be written in the Celtic idiom (some of which have been collected by David Adam).

Many people, such as myself, who in their student days were able to maintain the habit of a daily 'quiet time' for prayer and Bible study at the start of the day, find such a pattern of life impossible to maintain having begun work, got married, or had a family. The pattern of life then has to change to ensure that Bible study and prayer occur elsewhere in the weekly routine. However an act of prayer at the very start of the day is a uniquely potent practice in the fostering of a consciousness of God throughout the activity of the day. It is an act of acknowledgement of God and one of self-dedication.

This is the function of the Celtic *lorica* or 'breastplate prayer'. Here below is the Lorica of St Fursa which dates from the ninth century:

> May the yoke of the Law of God be upon this Shoulder,
> The coming of the Holy Spirit on this Head,
> The sign of Christ on this Forehead,
> The hearing of the Holy Spirit in these Ears,
> The smelling of the Holy Spirit in this Nose,
> The vision that the people of Heaven have in these Eyes,
> The speech of the people of Heaven in this Mouth,
> The work of the Church of God in these Hands,
> The good of God and of neighbour in these Feet.
> May God dwell in this Heart,
> And this Person belong entirely to God the Father.'

In dedicating the whole body to the Holy Trinity, we symbolically consecrate everything that makes us people.

Better known is the Lorica of St Patrick:

> Christ be with me, Christ within me,
> Christ behind me, Christ before me,
> Christ beside me, Christ to win me,
> Christ to comfort and restore me,
> Christ beneath me, Christ above me,
> Christ in quiet, Christ in danger,
> Christ in hearts of all that love me,
> Christ in mouth of friend and stranger.

The next two are taken from a collection of prayers recorded in the Outer Hebrides at the turn of this century:

God to enfold,
God to surround,
God in speech-told,
God my thought-bound.

God when I sleep,
God when I wake,
God my watch-keep,
God my hope-sake.

God my life-whole,
God lips apart,
God in my soul,
God in my heart.

God Wine and Bread,
God in my death,
God my soul-thread,
God ever breath.

Be the eye of God between me and each eye,
Between me and each purpose God's purpose lie,
Be the hand of God between me and each hand,
Between me and each shield the shield of God stand,
God's desire between me and each desire be,
Be God's bridle between each bridle and me,
   And no man's mouth able to curse me I see.

Between me and each pain the pain of Christ show,
Between me and each love the love of Christ grow,
Between me and each dearness Christ's dearness stay,
Christ's kindness between me and each kindness aye,
Between me and each wish the wish of Christ found,
Between me and each will the will of Christ bound,
   And no venom can wound me, make me unsound.[4]

Or for a slightly more modern prayer:

God be in my head and in my understanding.
God be in my eyes and in my looking.
God be in my mouth and in my speaking.
God be in my heart and in my thinking.
God be at my end and at my departing.

There are scores of such prayers, both ancient and modern, in the Celtic tradition. They can be easily used at the beginning of the day as a prayer of attention. They are easily integrated into even the most hectic schedule. For instance to pray slowly and attentively the Lorica of St Fursa takes little over one minute!

Celtic spirituality has much to teach about being conscious of God. In the use of such prayers, it can teach us to turn to God almost constantly and wake up to his constant presence with us in our every movement and action. As Avery Brooke writes:

> In this practice we have something that is . . . attainable today (. . . if we are willing to work at it . . .) and may sustain us through good times and bad times as it sustained the Celtic Christians so long ago.[5]

# 20

# CONCLUSION: DEPARTURE FROM ARRIVAL

> *Growth in prayer has no end.*
> THEOPHAN THE RECLUSE

One of the pictures that I use in my devotions is a postcard reproduction of Hobbema's *The Avenue*. It depicts a long dirt-road leading through an avenue of trees and off into the distance. The truth that this picture reminds me of is the nature of the Christian life as journey or pilgrimage. The picture reminds me that the goal of my desert journey is a long way off. Now that might, at first, seem a rather negative or discouraging thing to want to dwell on. But in fact I find this reminder profoundly encouraging. If I thought for one moment that I was anywhere near my destination, I would be worried. If I believed that in my life as it is, I was experiencing the goal of the Christian life, I would probably give up immediately! If I were to evaluate the Christian life purely on the basis of my own experience to date, what a meagre picture that would paint! *The Avenue* says to me, 'Don't worry, Paul; you haven't arrived; there's more to come!'

Too often people confuse the idea of having arrived, with the doctrine and experience of assurance. This is a very important doctrine in the Christian tradition, and one rooted in the Scriptures:

> Truly, truly I say to you, he who hears my word and believes him who sent me, has eternal life; he does not come into judgement, but has passed out of death into life. (John 5.24 RSV)
> Because of his great love for us, God, who is rich in mercy, made us alive in Christ, even when we were dead in transgressions—it is by grace you have been saved. And God

raised us up with Christ and seated us with him in the heavenly realms in Christ Jesus. (Ephesians 2.4–6)

Similarly, Colossians speaks of the believer's life being already 'hidden with Christ in God'. But does all this imagery mean that I have 'arrived'? Paradoxically it doesn't.

Indeed it is balanced by another image which occurs repeatedly throughout the New Testament. It's the image of the Christian life as a race. In the letter to the Hebrews, for example, we are exhorted to 'run with perseverance the race marked out for us' (Hebrews 12.1b) Similarly in 1 Corinthians St Paul writes:

> Do you not know that in a race all the runners run but only one gets the prize? Everyone who competes in the games goes into strict training. They do it to get a crown that will not last, but we do it to get a crown that will last forever. Therefore I do not run like a man running aimlessly; I do not fight like a man beating the air. No, I beat my body and make it my slave so that after I have preached to others, I myself will not be disqualified for the prize (1 Corinthians 9.24–27).

The same idea of pressing on towards the goal is found in Paul's letter to the Philippians:

> I want to know Christ and the power of his resurrection and the fellowship of sharing in his sufferings, becoming like him in his death, and so, somehow, to attain to the resurrection from the dead. Not that I have already obtained all this, or have already been made perfect, but I press on to take hold of that for which Christ Jesus took hold of me. Brothers I do not consider myself yet to have taken hold of it. But one thing I do: Forgetting what is behind and straining towards what is ahead, I press on towards the goal to win the prize for which God has called me heavenwards in Christ Jesus. (Philippians 3.10–14)

The Christian life is not—and never has been—a soft option. Following Christ has always been the harder choice, the narrow road. To live the Christian life demands perseverance and single-mindedness. The language of spiritual formation throughout the Bible is of struggle and movement.

In the very earliest years of the Church's history, both Christ and the Christian religion were referred to as 'the Way'. Indeed it was an idiom already in use by the time Acts was written. The word can mean either a journey or the roadway itself. Being united with Christ—the Way—inescapably means that we are going on a journey. It is a journey of revelation, of discovery; of becoming ourselves in God and growing in our participation in him.

Sometimes the Way is easy, and sometimes it is hard. At one stage I seem to be climbing a rough and steep hill, the next the road becomes flat and smooth. The Way will take us sometimes by still waters and green pastures, and sometimes through wastelands and desert places. I believe that Christ is with us every step of the journey, in the most profound way. But at times this everliving presence is invisible and hidden from us.

I may stumble and falter and show myself to be a very weak and inadequate pilgrim, and I may despair, from time to time, at the spiritual state of my life. But Hobbema's picture always serves to remind me that I have scarcely begun to follow Christ; that this is not all there is; my life is not the perfect fulfilment of Christianity; there is further to go and more to come. Thank goodness!

So we must not think of the Christian life as a state of arrival. There are some senses in which we might use such terms: as those in Christ, we *have* found the way of salvation, we *have* received the Holy Spirit as a 'deposit', we *have* access to God in prayer. Yes, an arrival has happened. But there is more to give and to receive; always further to go. Union with Christ the Way can only mean to be on a journey. We could think of the Christian life, then, as a departure from an arrival. There is some way between what we have received and what we shall receive, between the current reality and future fulfilment, between the now and the not yet.

In the meantime, says St Paul, we 'groan inwardly' as we await our final redemption. Indeed there are times when we are only too aware of the groaning aspect of the Christian life! There are long tracts of the journey in which God seems to be quite absent. This can only be an apparent or 'sensory' absence. For if it is within God that we live and move and have our being, then his real or radical absence would inevitably signal our extinction. Nonetheless from the point of view of our own experience, God is often not to be found. And this is one of the central motifs to the desert experience.

## PUSHING ON

Sometimes the pilgrim does not realize that he or she is undergoing a desert experience or a dark night. It is sometimes another person, a pastor or a spiritual director who discerns what God is doing in the person. Indeed it is at the period of transition that having a spiritual director can be most helpful and important. For the individual may well be coming onto unfamiliar territory. Leonard Griffith tells the following story:

> There was once a graduate student at Oxford who came away from his supervisor's office feeling dreadfully despondent. The supervisor told him that he had exhausted all the available English literature on the subject and would now have to read the untranslated works of German scholars. 'But Sir,' the student protested, 'I don't know German.' With Oxford casualness, the supervisor replied, 'Then it would seem that you will have to take time out to learn it. You have gone as far as you can otherwise.'[1]

In this story Leonard Griffith has provided us with a positive way of understanding the desert experience. The desert experience is in a sense the opportunity to go further with God, to make a new thrust, to learn a new spiritual language.

Of course so long as we believe that we have Christianity wrapped up or that we have arrived, we will not see the need for such new thrusts. But we cannot mature so long as we believe we already are mature. We cannot be truly wise until we acknowledge our ignorance. If our knowledge of God is to live and grow, we must acknowledge its need to grow, that is we must face up to and admit our own unknowing or lack of knowledge. This is the beginning of true knowledge which leads to union with God.

We are like a man standing on a beach at the water's edge, holding a candle at the dark of night. And we ask, 'Has he seen the ocean?' If he knows the limitedness of his ability to see, then yes in a sense he has seen the ocean. If he is not aware that his vision is limited, then he will not have seen the ocean. He will have seen a few shallow waves lapping the beach, and he will have mistaken that for the ocean!

Like this man, we must not let our partial knowledge of God become a barrier to greater knowledge of him. God will always remain incomprehensible to us; unknowing will always remain a part of our relationship with him. It is only if we embrace this unknowing and acknowledge that we pray to a God whom we do not know or understand that we can achieve union with him and see him more truly as he is.

The anonymous fourteenth-century author of *The Cloud of Unknowing* put it this way:

> Try as you might, this darkness and this cloud (of unknowing) will remain between you and your God. You will feel frustrated because your mind will be unable to grasp him . . . But learn to be at home in this darkness . . . for, if in this life you hope to feel and see God as he is in himself, it must be within this darkness and this cloud.[2]

Our certainty as Christian disciples is that our ultimate goal is also our ultimate reality; we follow Christ both *in* and *toward* union with God. We know the destination. And so we call our whole life a pilgrimage. We know the destination but not the detail of the route. In the words of the writer to the Hebrews, 'it is Christ who leads us in our faith and brings it to perfection.' (Hebrews 12.2 NJB) Ours is to follow in the unknowing of faith.

When Thomas objected, 'Lord, we don't know where you are going, so how can we know the way?' Jesus replied, 'I am the way, and the truth and the life!' (John 14.5,6). Like Thomas we have to follow in the darkness of faith. This pursuit will bring us through unfamiliar and sometimes hostile territory. Christ the Way will sometimes bring us to cool streams and green places, and at other times to the desert wilderness. But it is often in the desert that we learn the most and that God is best able to transform us. In the words of Kenneth Leech:

> The desert is the place where idols are smashed, illusions are unmasked and where the human heart is exposed . . . Only through such pain and upheaval can maturity come.[3]

This is hard, bewildering and unpleasant stuff. But it is there in the desert that we learn to become ourselves in God. It will be in the wilderness that we learn for ourselves how to make prayer living, and how to keep it alive. I hope that perhaps through this book you will have found some ways to do this. The desert, or the dark night, can feel a sad and lonely place, and so I hope that you now realize that you really are in good company!

I shall sign off with some words of Julian of Norwich, which have been a great encouragement to me in just such times. I'll quote it first in modern English:

> Pray inwardly, even if you do not enjoy it. It does good even though you think you are doing nothing. For when you are dry, empty, sick, or weak, at such a time your prayer is most

pleasing to me, though you find little enough to enjoy in it. This is true of all believing prayer.[4]

I shall now quote it in an earlier form, which brings out a different timbre, and lends a richness and a resonance to these words of God's unimaginable grace and simple kindness:

Pray inwardly,
Though thou thinkest it savour thee not.
For it is profitable
Though thou feel not
Though thou see not
Yea, even though thou thinkest thou canst not.
For in dryness and in barrenness,
In sickness and in feebleness,
Then is thy prayer well pleasant to me,
Though thou thinkest it savour thee nought but little,
And so is all thy believing prayer in my sight.

# NOTES

CHAPTER 1: PRAYER 'IN THE PITS'
1  St John of the Cross, *Selected Writings*, SPCK 1987
2  Theophan the Recluse, *The Art of Prayer*, Faber 1966
3  Metropolitan Anthony of Sourozh, *School for Prayer*, DLT 1970. This book, with *Living Prayer, Courage to Pray* and *God and Man*, is included in *The Essence of Prayer*, DLT 1986.

CHAPTER 2: PRAYING FRANKLY
1  Nels F.S. Ferre, *Making Religion Real*, Fontana 1969
2  Alastair V. Campbell, *Rediscovering Pastoral Care*, DLT 1981
3  Kenneth Leech, *Spirituality and Pastoral Care*, Sheldon 1986
4  Kenneth Leech, *ibid.*
5  Dom Lorenzo Scupoli, *The Spiritual Combat*, Methuen 1909

CHAPTER 3: EDUCATING THE AFFECTIONS
1  St Francis de Sales, *Introduction to the Devout Life*, McGrath
2  St Francis de Sales, *ibid.*

CHAPTER 4: LOVING GOD
1  Thomas à Kempis, *The Imitation of Christ*, a modern reading by Bernard Langley, Highland 1983
2  Richard of St Victor, *Of the Four Degrees of Passionate Love*, McGrath
3  Archimandrite Sophrony, *The Monk of Mount Athos*, Mowbrays 1973
4  Gary R. Collins, *The 60 Second Christian*, Word 1984
5  St John of the Cross, *Selected Writings*

CHAPTER 5: AIMING FOR GOD
1  Valentine Zandar, *The Life of St Seraphim*, The Fellowship of St Alban and St Sergius
2  Sergius Bolshakoff, *Russian Mystics*, Cistercian Publications 1980
3  tr. Jane Ellis, *An Early Soviet Saint, the life of Father Zachariah*, Templegate 1977

## CHAPTER 6: THE DARK NIGHT

1 Metropolitan Anthony of Sourozh, *School for Prayer*, DLT 1970
2 St John of the Cross, *Selected Writings*
3 Archimandrite Sophrony, *His Life is Mine*, Mowbrays
4 Kenneth Leech, *Spirituality and Pastoral Care*

## CHAPTER 7: THE WAY OF INTEGRATION

1 Paul Tillich, *The Shaking of the Foundations*, Penguin 1962
2 David Watson, *I Believe in the Church*, Hodder 1978
3 David Adam, *The Edge of Glory*, Triangle 1985
4 Metropolitan Anthony of Sourozh, *The Essence of Prayer*

## CHAPTER 8: BEING REAL

1 Richard Woods, *Eckhart's Way*, DLT 1987
2 St John of the Cross, *Selected Writings*
3 Metropolitan Anthony of Sourozh, *Courage to Pray*, DLT 1973
4 Metropolitan Anthony of Sourozh, *ibid.*

## CHAPTER 9: BEING IMPOLITE

1 Theophan the Recluse, *The Art of Prayer*

## CHAPTER 10: BEING DETACHED

1 Kenneth Leech, *Spirituality and Pastoral Care*
2 Thomas Merton, *Thoughts in Solitude*, Burns and Oates 1975

## CHAPTER 12: BRIDGING WORK

1 Brother Lawrence, *The Practice of the Presence of God*, Epworth 1959
2 Metropolitan Anthony of Sourozh, *School for Prayer*
3 David Adam, *The Edge of Glory*

## CHAPTER 13: BRIDGING NOISE

1 tr. R.M. French, *The Way of a Pilgrim*, Triangle 1986
2 *The Alternative Service Book 1980*
3 David Adam, *The Edge of Glory*

## CHAPTER 14: THE PRAYER OF ATTENTION

1 Metropolitan Anthony, *Living Prayer*, DLT 1966
2 tr. R.M. French, *The Way of a Pilgrim*
3 Metropolitan Anthony, *School for Prayer*

CHAPTER 16: PRAYING WITH HEAVEN
1   The Liturgy of the CSWG, the Monastery of the Holy Trinity, Crawley Down

CHAPTER 17: STIMULATING PRAYER
1   Thomas à Kempis, *The Imitation of Christ*

CHAPTER 19: GOD-CONSCIOUSNESS
1   Richard Woods, *Eckhart's Way*
2   Archimandrite Sophrony, *His Life is Mine*
3   Avery Brooke, *Celtic Prayers*, Seabury 1980
4   G.R.D. McLean, *Praying with Highland Christians*, Triangle 1988
5   Avery Brooke, *Celtic Prayers*

CHAPTER 20: CONCLUSION—DEPARTURE FROM ARRIVAL
1   Leonard Griffith, *God in Man's Experience*, Hodder 1968
2   *The Cloud of Unknowing*, tr. Halcyon Backhouse, Hodder 1985
3   Kenneth Leech, *Spirituality and Pastoral Care*
4   Julian of Norwich, *Revelations of Divine Love*, tr. Clifton Wolters, Penguin 1966

## THE EDGE OF GLORY
*Prayers in the Celtic Tradition*
### by David Adam

Modern prayers which recapture the Celtic way of prayer, intertwining the divine glory with the ordinariness of everyday life. Beautifully illustrated with Celtic patterns and line drawings.

## THE CRY OF THE DEER
*Meditations on the hymn of St Patrick*
### by David Adam

David Adam continues to explore the Celtic way of prayer in a series of meditations leading into practical exercises, all based on the hymn, 'St Patrick's Breastplate'.

## TIDES AND SEASONS
*Modern prayers in the Celtic Tradition*
### by David Adam

From the rich store of Celtic spirituality David Adam draws insights which speak to us directly. His prayers and meditations echo the rhythms of creation which find their parallel in our spiritual lives.

## THE EYE OF THE EAGLE
*Meditations on the hymn 'Be thou my vision'*
### by David Adam

David Adam takes us through this popular hymn, discovering the spiritual riches that are hidden in all our lives. He includes exercises so that we can experience the vision for ourselves.

## The PRAYING WITH series

A series of books making accessible the words of some of the
great characters and traditions of faith for use by all Christians.

PRAYING WITH SAINT AUGUSTINE
Introduction by Murray Watts

PRAYING WITH SAINT FRANCIS
Introduction by David Ford

PRAYING WITH HIGHLAND CHRISTIANS
Introduction by Sally Magnusson

PRAYING WITH THE NEW TESTAMENT
Introduction by Joyce Huggett

PRAYING WITH SAINT TERESA
Introduction by Elaine Storkey

PRAYING WITH THE JEWISH TRADITION
Introduction by Lionel Blue

PRAYING WITH THE OLD TESTAMENT
Introduction by Richard Holloway

PRAYING WITH THE ORTHODOX TRADITION
Preface by Kallistos Ware

PRAYING WITH THE ENGLISH HYMN WRITERS
Compiled and Introduced by Timothy Dudley-Smith

PRAYING WITH THE ENGLISH MYSTICS
Compiled and Introduced by Jenny Robertson

PRAYING WITH THE ENGLISH TRADITION
Compiled and Introduced by Margaret Pawley

PRAYING WITH THE ENGLISH POETS
Compiled and Introduced by Ruth Etchells